Joint Development of Offshore Oil and Gas Resources in the Arctic Ocean Region and the United Nations Convention on the Law of the Sea

The Law of the Sea

Volumes published in this Brill Research Perspectives title are listed at *brill.com/rpls*

Joint Development of Offshore Oil and Gas Resources in the Arctic Ocean Region and the United Nations Convention on the Law of the Sea

By

John Abrahamson

BRILL

LEIDEN | BOSTON

This paperback book edition is simultaneously published as issue 1.4 (2017) of *Law of the Sea*, DOI:10.1163/24519359-12340004.

Library of Congress Control Number: 2018952493

Typeface for the Latin, Greek, and Cyrillic scripts: "Brill". See and download: brill.com/brill-typeface

ISBN 978-90-04-38009-7 (paperback)
ISBN 978-90-04-38010-3 (e-book)

This book is printed on acid-free paper and produced in a sustainable manner.

Contents

Author Biography

John Abrahamson
has over 30 years' international taxation experience specialising in upstream oil and gas and related international treaties, including General Manager International Tax, Maersk Oil and Gas (Denmark), International Tax Partner, Sheltons-SITTI (Denmark), Structured Finance Executive, Commonwealth Bank of Australia (Sydney and Malta), Senior Tax Associate, Baker & McKenzie (Melbourne), and Tax Manager, Arthur Andersen and KPMG (Hong Kong). John wrote *Tolley's International Taxation of Upstream Oil and Gas* (1st Edition, LexisNexis, 2014, 2nd Edition, LexisNexis, 2017), *Tolley's International Taxation of Corporate Finance* (LexisNexis, 2014), *International Taxation of Manufacturing and Distribution* (Kluwer Law, 2016) and *International Taxation of Energy Production and Distribution* (Kluwer Law, 2018). He has presented courses on international taxation in London, Aberdeen, Jersey, Paris, Amsterdam, Copenhagen, Rotterdam, Zurich, Lugano, Warsaw, Cyprus, Sydney, Melbourne, Brisbane, Perth, Hong Kong, Singapore, Kuala Lumpur, Seoul, Sao Paulo, Rio de Janeiro, Mexico City and Houston. John has a Ph.D. from the ANU College of Law and is a Chartered Tax Adviser.

Joint Development of Offshore Oil and Gas Resources in the Arctic Ocean Region and the United Nations Convention on the Law of the Sea

John Abrahamson
Partner, Sheltons-SITTI
J.Abrahamson@Sheltonsgroup.com

Abstract

The Arctic Ocean region presents certain challenges to peaceful cooperation between states, particularly in the locations where ocean boundaries and ownership of the related resources are disputed. The establishment of Joint Development Zones (JDZs) for the development of offshore oil and gas resources in the Arctic Ocean can facilitate international cooperation over resource development where there are competing claims. These claims are generally based on continental shelf jurisdiction under the provisions of the United Nations Convention on the Law of the Sea (UNCLOS). There are several alternative dispute resolution measures available under UNCLOS; however, a number of states have preferred to adopt a JDZ as an interim measure to allow development. The significance of JDZs for the Arctic Ocean region is that they can allow peaceful cooperation and development where the specific circumstances of Arctic claims make it difficult for the respective states to agree on the maritime boundary.

Keywords

international law – sea boundaries – Arctic – joint development – upstream oil and gas

1 Introduction

Joint Development Zones (JDZs) are a means where states agree to share resources of a disputed region. JDZs are of special interest in relation to the Arctic Ocean region owing to the number of unresolved maritime boundaries

 | DOI:10.1163/9789004380103_002

in the region, and the recent extension of maritime claims by Arctic states. JDZs are agreements between states to allow the sharing of benefits from offshore oil and gas production, and so they effectively suspend disputes over sovereignty of an offshore region. They are increasingly used to allow international cooperation where there are boundary disputes, particularly where the existing terms of the United Nations Convention on the Law of the Sea (UNCLOS)[1] can give rise to competing claims.

One definition of joint development has been offered by Ian Townsend-Gault and is as follows:[2]

> ... a decision by one or more countries to pool any rights they may have over a given area and, to a greater or lesser degree, undertake some form of joint management for the purposes of exploring and exploiting offshore minerals.

This definition includes JDZs adopted pending the future settlement of a maritime boundary, and JDZs where states have agreed a maritime boundary, but have also agreed to share resources of a JDZ. The definition can also include multilateral agreements, which allow access to resources by more than two states. There have been several other definitions of joint development. Rainer Lagoni defined joint development as follows:[3]

> ... the cooperation between states with regard to the exploration for and exploitation of certain deposits, fields or accumulations of non-living resources which either extend beyond a boundary or lie in areas of overlapping claims.

The definition includes unitisation agreements where boundaries are agreed. The Townsend-Gault definition may, however, be somewhat more precise by referring to the pooling of rights, and the use of joint management to a greater or lesser extent. Masahiro Miyoshi defined joint development as follows:[4]

1 1982 United Nations Convention on the Law of the Sea, 1833 *UNTS* 396 (hereafter UNCLOS).

2 Ian Townsend-Gault, 'Joint Development of Offshore Mineral Resources – Progress and Prospects for the Future' (1988) 12(3) *Natural Resources Forum* 275 at p. 275.

3 Rainer Lagoni, 'Oil and Gas Deposits across National Frontiers' (1979) 73(2) *American Journal of International Law* 215 at p. 215.

4 Masahiro Miyoshi and Clive H. Schofield (eds), 'The Joint Development of Offshore Oil and Gas in relation to Maritime Boundary Delimitation' (1999) 2(5) *IBRU Maritime Briefing* 3.

> … an inter-governmental arrangement of a provisional nature, designed for functional purposes of joint exploration for and/or exploitation of hydrocarbon resources of the sea-bed beyond the territorial sea.

This definition excludes joint ventures between governments and oil companies, and is intended to focus on arrangements where resources are shared between two or more states. The agreement focused on joint development as provisional arrangements pending a settlement, in accordance with UNCLOS Article 83.

Hazel Fox adopts a definition which focusses on bilateral agreements. This was used for the analysis of a Model Agreement for joint development between two states:[5]

> … an agreement between two states to develop so as to share jointly in agreed proportions by inter-state cooperation and national measures the offshore oil and gas in a designated zone of the seabed and subsoil of the continental shelf to which both or either of the participating states are entitled in international law.

Fox referred to multilateral JDZ regimes, including the 1988 Convention on the Regulation of Antarctic Mineral Resource Activities (CRAMRA) and the Area under Part XI of UNCLOS, although the focus of Fox's analysis was the development of a bilateral Model JDZ agreement.

The definition used by Townsend-Gault will be adopted in this study because this broader definition can include permanent and multilateral regimes for sharing of offshore oil and gas resources which can apply in the Arctic Ocean region.

JDZs have been introduced in a significant number of ocean areas: from seas subject to ice conditions, to seas adjacent to desert regions, JDZs between two states, and also multilateral regimes which involve several states. JDZs have been developed in relation to boundary disputes arising from different historical and geographical circumstances, and may therefore show potential to be adapted to circumstances in the Arctic Ocean region. JDZs have also been developed with different regimes for jurisdictional control and resource sharing. Other forms of multilateral development have also been established, such as the Area regime, under Part XI of UNCLOS.

5 Hazel Fox et al, *Joint Development of Offshore Oil and Gas: A Model Agreement for States for Joint Development with Explanatory Commentary* (British Institute of International and Comparative Law, London: 1989) 45 and 54.

The JDZ examples used in several locations principally relate to oil and gas resources, which have historically been the most valuable non-living resources. JDZs may also relate to other resources such as fish stocks. The use of JDZs may be suitable in the future for other resources such as rare-earth elements (REE)[6] or biological compounds and genetic materials used in pharmaceuticals.[7]

Access to Arctic Ocean resources may increase owing to global warming, with a significant rise in global temperatures likely to reduce ice congestion in the Arctic Ocean region.[8] Technological developments in oil and gas extraction and transportation may also allow increasing access to potential resources in the Arctic Ocean region. This may also allow access to hydrocarbons existing in extremely cold climates which are trapped in forms other than oil or gas, such as gas hydrates.[9]

Research on the full potential of offshore oil and gas in the Arctic Ocean region is underway, including offshore drilling programmes on the United States Alaskan coast and the Russian Siberian coast.[10] Reports to date indicate that very large potential oil and gas fields may be present, based on sedimentary basins, as discussed by Macnab, Paul Neto and Rob van de Poll.[11] Green and Kaplan considered that the significant part of oil and gas reserves in the sedimentary basins of the Arctic may be within the 200-nautical-mile EEZ of the states with coastlines.[12] Michael D Max and Allan Lowrie have commented that large reserves of natural gas hydrates in the Arctic Ocean basin may exist outside the 200-nautical-mile EEZ limit.

Kenneth J Bird and his colleagues of the United States Geological Survey (USGS) issued the Circum-Arctic Resource Appraisal (CARA) Estimates of

6 'In a hole? Demand for some rare-earth elements could rapidly outstrip supply', *The Economist* (17 March 2012) at: http://www.economist.com/node/21550243 (last accessed 1 March 2018).

7 Donald R Rothwell and Tim Stephens, *The International Law of the Sea* 2nd ed (Hart Publishing, Oxford: 2016) 355.

8 Intergovernmental Panel on Climate Change, 'Working Group I Contribution to the IPCC Fifth Assessment Report, Climate Change 2013: The Physical Science Basis', at: http://www.ipcc.ch (last accessed 1 March 2018).

9 Gas hydrates are gases, such as methane, trapped in structures resembling ice.

10 For a general summary of current Arctic oil and gas developments see: Ernst & Young, *Arctic Oil and Gas* (2013) at: http://www.ourenergypolicy.org/wp-content/uploads/2013/09/Arctic_oil_and_gas.pdf (last accessed 3 April 2018).

11 Ron Macnab, Paul Neto and Rob van de Poll, 'Cooperative Preparations for Determining the Outer Limit of the Juridical Continental Shelf in the Arctic Ocean' (2001) *Boundary and Security Bulletin* 86.

12 Arthur R Green and Anatoly A Kaplan, 'The Geological Framework and Hydrocarbon Potential of Sedimentary Basins of the Arctic', in *Proceedings of the Twelfth World Petroleum Congress* Vol 2 (1987) 79.

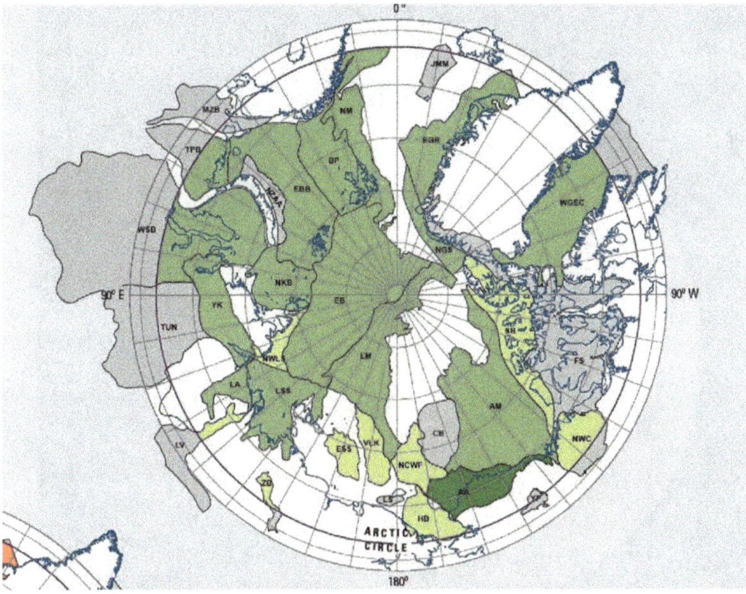

FIGURE 1 Potential arctic oil regions
SOURCE: UNITED STATES GEOLOGICAL SURVEY
DEPARTMENT OF THE INTERIOR/USGS

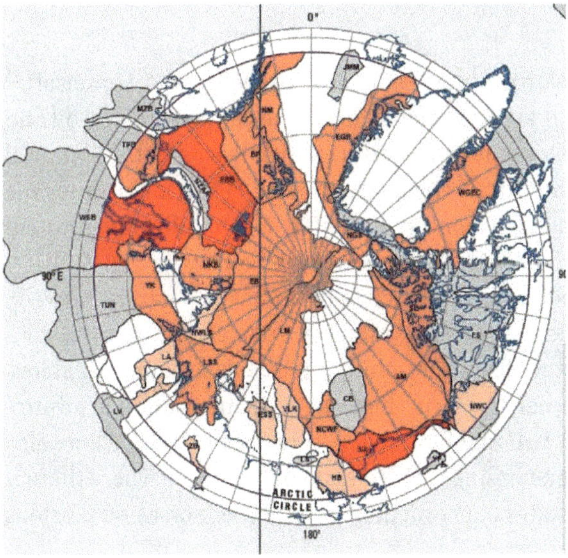

FIGURE 2 Potential arctic gas regions
SOURCE: UNITED STATES GEOLOGICAL SURVEY
DEPARTMENT OF THE INTERIOR/USGS

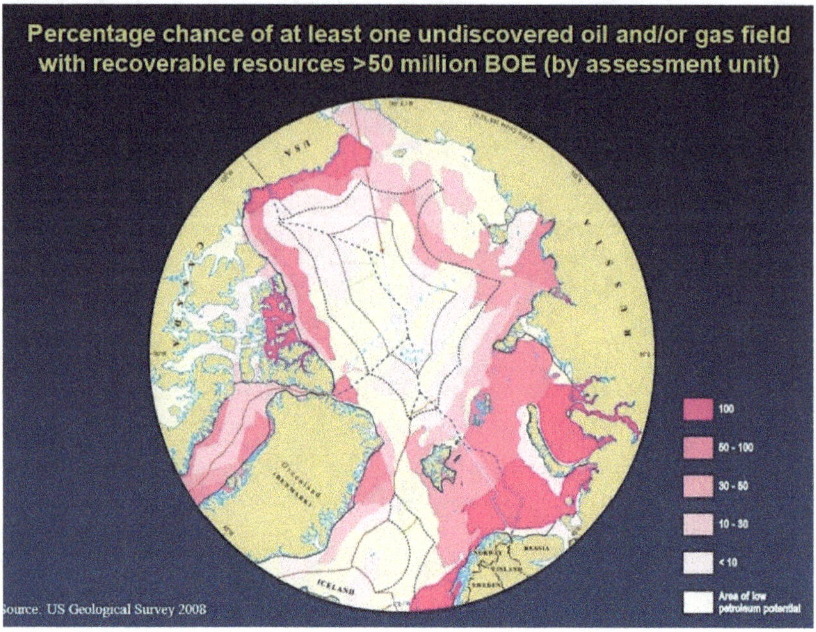

FIGURE 3 Potential arctic gas regions overlaid with arctic boundary claims
SOURCE: IBRU, DURHAM UNIVERSITY, UK HTTPS://WWW.DUR.AC.UK/IBRU/RESOURCES/ARCTIC/ © COPYRIGHT 2018 IBRU: CENTRE FOR BORDERS RESEARCH

Undiscovered Oil and Gas North of the Arctic Circle in 2008 (USGS Appraisal).[13] These surveys are important because they indicate the very substantial oil and gas potential in the Arctic Ocean region. Figure 1 illustrates the USGS Appraisal of potential oil regions in the Arctic Ocean region, and Figure 2 illustrates the USGS Appraisal of potential gas regions in the region. Figure 3 illustrates potential oil and gas regions overlaid with Arctic boundary claims.

The use of JDZs is one potential approach to promote cooperation between states in regions of potential boundary conflicts. JDZs should also be considered in the context of the dispute resolution methods available to states, particularly the International Court of Justice (ICJ), international arbitration, and the International Tribunal for the Law of the Sea (ITLOS). There also needs to be a realistic understanding that JDZs can only be used where there is continued support of the states concerned. In view of the increasing tensions

13 Kenneth J Bird et al, 'Circum-Arctic Resource Appraisal: Estimates of Undiscovered Oil and Gas North of the Arctic Circle', *U.S. Geological Survey Fact Sheet* (2008–3049) at: http://pubs.usgs.gov/fs/2008/3049/ (last accessed 2 March 2018).

between certain states in the Arctic Ocean region, it is timely to examine the potential use of JDZs in relation to current conflicts in the region.

This study introduces the governance framework relating to Arctic Ocean region maritime boundaries, including the Law of the Sea, dispute resolution, the Commission on the Limits of the Continental Shelf, the International Seabed Authority, and the Arctic Council. The Arctic Ocean maritime boundaries and related disputes are then examined. The basis of JDZs is analysed, with selected examples with similarities to the Arctic Ocean region. The JDZ implementation issues for the Arctic Ocean region are then reviewed. This analysis will establish the strong basis to consider use of JDZs in relation to a number of current Arctic Ocean boundary disputes.

The geographical scope of this study is based on the regions currently subject to sea-ice conditions, and includes regions in general proximity to the Arctic Circle extending to the North Pole, including the Bering, Chukchi, Beaufort, Greenland, Norwegian and Barents Seas.[14]

2 Arctic Legal Framework and Governance

The Arctic Ocean region is characterised by several developing governance regimes, commencing with the general framework of the law of the sea, comprising specific topics, including: dispute resolution and the mechanisms available to resolve maritime boundary disputes, the Commission on the Limits of the Continental Shelf (CLCS), which is currently evaluating continental shelf claims by several Arctic states, and the International Seabed Authority (ISBA) which will manage the mineral resources in the regions of the Arctic Ocean which will be beyond state claims under the Area regime of UNCLOS Part XI. The governance regimes include regional developments outside of the law of the sea, in particular the development of the Arctic Council, which is formulating an increasing role in regional cooperation, development, and protection of the Arctic environment.

2.1 *The Law of the Sea – The General Framework*

UNCLOS provides the essential framework for maritime boundary delimitation under the current law of the sea. The historical development of maritime zones and related boundary delimitation and dispute resolution provisions are

14 The analysis will include the continental shelf claims in this region, comprising the United States, Canada, Denmark (based on Denmark's claim to Greenland), Iceland, Norway (including the Svalbard Islands) and Russia.

analysed below. A significant issue is that certain circumstances give rise to boundary disputes, notwithstanding UNCLOS maritime boundary provisions.

Maritime boundaries have historically been determined by treaties, with the practice of referring disputes to arbitration commencing in the early twentieth century. The evolution of maritime boundaries has had to address the development of new zones, including continental shelf zones, originally provided for by the 1958 Convention on the Continental Shelf,[15] which can now extend up to or beyond 350 nautical miles under the UNCLOS and the EEZ regime extending to 200 nautical miles from the coastal state, also provided for in UNCLOS. The development of these zones has increased the length of boundaries to be determined and significantly increased the ocean areas under the jurisdiction of states.

There is a threshold issue relevant to Arctic Ocean maritime boundaries: whether the provisions of UNCLOS relating to maritime zones and their related rights and responsibilities are binding on states which have not ratified the convention, on the basis that they are incorporated into customary international law. In relation to the Arctic Ocean region, this issue only relates to the United States which has neither signed nor acceded to UNCLOS. In this respect, decisions of the International Court of Justice (ICJ) have held that specific terms of UNCLOS, such as the definition of the continental shelf set out in Article 76, paragraph 1, form part of customary international law.[16] On this basis UNCLOS maritime boundaries are likely to be binding on the United States.

The principal sea zone which is typically subject to JDZ arrangements is the continental shelf. The continental shelf under UNCLOS is defined under Article 76, and 'comprises the sea-bed and subsoil of the submarine areas that extend beyond ... [a state's] territorial sea throughout the natural prolongation of its land territory to the outer edge of the continental margin, or to a distance of 200 nautical miles ...'[17] That part of the continental shelf beyond 200 nautical miles has been described as the outer continental shelf. The coastal state's continental shelf claim beyond 200 nautical miles must be submitted to the CLCS. The Commission is required to make recommendations to coastal States on matters relating to the establishment of the outer limits of

15 1958 Convention on the Continental Shelf, 499 *UNTS* 312.

16 For example, see *Territorial Dispute and Maritime Delimitation* (Nicaragua v. Colombia) [2012] ICJ Rep 624, 666 and 669.

17 Article 76(1), UNCLOS.

their continental shelf. The limits of the shelf established by the coastal State on the basis of the recommendations are final and binding.[18]

The 'Outer Limit Line' is the limit of the continental shelf where it naturally extends beyond 200 nautical miles, and is based on the foot of slope feature on the seabed floor, plus the greater of:

i) The line where the sediment thickness on the seabed floor is 1% of the distance to the foot of slope; or,
ii) 60 nautical miles from the foot of slope.[19]

This distance is then limited to the greater of:

i) The 2500 meter isobath (water depth line) plus 100 nautical miles; or,
ii) The territorial sea baseline plus 350 nautical miles.[20]

The continental shelf is limited to 350 nautical miles in respect of submarine ridges, however, this limit does not apply to 'submarine elevations that are natural components of the continental margin, such as its plateaux, rises, caps, banks and spurs'.[21]

The coastal state exercises sovereign rights over the continental shelf for the purpose of exploring it and exploiting its natural resources.[22] The coastal state has the exclusive right to authorise and regulate drilling on the continental shelf.[23] The coastal state is required under Article 82 to make payments or contributions in kind in respect of the exploitation of the non-living resources of the continental shelf beyond 200 nautical miles. The payments are made to the ISBA, which is required to distribute these amounts to states party to UNCLOS on the basis of 'equitable sharing criteria, taking into account the interests and needs of developing states, particularly the least developed and the land-locked among them.'[24]

The continental shelf regime overlaps the EEZ regime in certain respects up to 200 nautical miles.[25] The EEZ and continental shelf regimes both give sovereign rights to mineral and other non-living resources and sedentary fish resources up to 200 nautical miles from the coastal state baseline. The EEZ regime gives broader related rights over fishing, pollution and scientific research.

---

18 Article 76(8), UNCLOS.
19 Article 76(4), UNCLOS.
20 Article 76(5), UNCLOS.
21 Article 76(6), UNCLOS.
22 Article 77(1), UNCLOS.
23 Article 81, UNCLOS.
24 Article 82(4), UNCLOS.
25 The continental regime overlaps the EEZ regime in certain respects up to 200 nautical miles.

The UNCLOS provides that 'Pending agreement as provided for in paragraph 1, the States concerned, in a spirit of understanding and cooperation, shall make every effort to enter into provisional arrangements of a practical nature and, during this transitional period, not to jeopardize or hamper the reaching of the final agreement. Such arrangements shall be without prejudice to the final delimitation.'[26] These arrangements can include the establishment of JDZs in cases where the maritime boundary has not been agreed.[27]

The EEZ is the second of the two principal sea zones subject to JDZs under UNCLOS. The EEZ is defined under Article 55 as the area from the coastal state's baseline extending beyond and adjacent to the territorial sea with a combination of rights and jurisdiction of the coastal State and the rights and freedoms of other States.[28] The EEZ does not extend beyond 200 nautical miles as measured from the territorial sea baselines.[29] The coastal state has sovereign rights within the EEZ for the purpose of exploring and exploiting, conserving and managing the living and non-living resources of the waters superjacent to the sea-bed, the sea-bed and its subsoil, and other activities for the economic exploitation and exploration of the zone.[30] The coastal state also has jurisdiction over artificial islands, installations and structures, marine scientific research, and the protection of the marine environment.[31] All states have rights of navigation and overflight, laying of submarine cables and pipelines, and other internationally lawful uses of the sea.[32] Accordingly, the EEZ is a zone conferring coastal state sovereign rights over living and non-living resources to the coastal state, while retaining all other high seas freedoms for all states.

An UNCLOS regime which has a potential relationship with JDZs is the 'Area' under Part XI.[33] The Area is defined as 'the sea-bed and ocean floor and subsoil thereof, beyond the limits of national jurisdiction.'[34] The Area is estimated to comprise 50 per cent of the earth's surface.[35] Part XI provides that the mineral resources beyond state jurisdiction are to be used to benefit all states, and

26 Article 83(3), UNCLOS.

27 Most JDZs do not delimit the maritime boundary, and therefore provide that the agreement shall not prejudice a future boundary delimitation agreement.

28 Article 55, UNCLOS.

29 Article 57, UNCLOS.

30 Article 56, UNCLOS.

31 Article 56, UNCLOS.

32 Article 58, UNCLOS.

33 Article 133, UNCLOS.

34 Article 1(1), UNCLOS.

35 Michael Lodge, 'The International Seabed Authority and Deep Seabed Mining', UN Chronicle (May 2017) LIV, No 1 and 2 *UN Chronicle*, at: https://unchronicle.un.org/article/

establishes a regime for exploitation of resources. The Area regime provides for multiple resource developments, in contrast to the common form of JDZ, which relates to particular development opportunities.

2.2 *Dispute Resolution and Maritime Boundary Delimitation*

UNCLOS has extensive provisions relating to dispute resolution, which can be used to obtain conciliation, arbitration or ICJ proceedings to establish a maritime boundary. In relation to the EEZ, Article 74(3) of UNCLOS requires States with opposite or adjacent coasts to make every effort to enter into provisional arrangements of a practical nature pending agreement on the final delimitation of the EEZ between them in a manner consistent with international law. In relation to the continental shelf, UNCLOS requires States with opposite or adjacent coasts to make every effort to enter into provisional arrangements of a practical nature, pending agreement on the final delimitation of the continental shelf between them, in a manner consistent with international law,[36] and on this basis the agreement to establish a JDZ is consistent with these UNCLOS provisional arrangement provisions.

If no agreement can be reached within a reasonable period of time, the States concerned shall resort to the procedures provided for in UNCLOS Part XV.[37] Part XV provides for the settlement of disputes on the basis that state parties shall settle any dispute between them concerning the interpretation or application of this Convention by peaceful means.[38] UNCLOS provides priority to state parties to agree at any time to settle a dispute between them by any peaceful means of their own choice.[39]

Dispute resolution is based on the initial obligation of the parties to exchange views.[40] A state party may invite the other party or parties to submit the dispute to conciliation in accordance with UNCLOS or another conciliation procedure.[41] Where no settlement has been reached under conciliation, the dispute may be submitted at the request of any party to the dispute to the court or tribunal having jurisdiction under UNCLOS.[42]

---

international-seabed-authority-and-deep-seabed-mining (last accessed 10 April 2018). The Area will then be the regions beyond all state continental shelf zones.

36 Article 83(3), UNCLOS.

37 Articles 74(2) and 83(2), UNCLOS.

38 Article 279, UNCLOS.

39 Article 280, UNCLOS.

40 Article 283, UNCLOS.

41 Article 284, UNCLOS.

42 Article 286, UNCLOS.

States are free to choose when signing, ratifying or acceding to UNCLOS or at any time thereafter from all or some of the following means for the settlement of disputes listed in Article 287:[43]

- The ITLOS established under Annex VI;
- The ICJ;
- An arbitral tribunal constituted under Annex VII; and
- A special arbitral tribunal constituted under Annex VIII for specific categories of disputes comprising fisheries, environmental protection and preservation, marine scientific research, and navigation, including pollution from vessels and dumping.

A state is, however, free when signing, ratifying or acceding to the Convention or at any time thereafter, to declare in writing under Article 298 that it does not accept any one or more of the procedures provided for specific categories of disputes, including 'disputes concerning the interpretation or application of articles 15, 74 and 83 relating to sea boundary delimitations'.[44] The UN Division for Ocean Affairs and the Law of the Sea (DOALOS) maintains a listing of the declarations, including the order of preference for dispute resolution and declarations that a particular method or methods are not accepted.[45] UNCLOS provides that a state party may be deemed to have accepted arbitration, and that if the parties to a dispute have not accepted the same procedure for the settlement of the dispute, it may be submitted only to arbitration unless the parties otherwise agree.[46] Arbitration may therefore have a 'residual compulsory role.'[47]

There is a related issue of compulsory conciliation. UNCLOS requires compulsory conciliation in relation to disputed maritime boundaries.[48] It is not possible for a state to opt out of these conciliation procedures. Although the findings of the conciliation commission are not binding, there is a requirement to inform the other party of the reasons for not adopting the recommendations.

---

43 Article 287, UNCLOS.

44 Article 298, UNCLOS.

45 United Nations Division for Ocean Affairs and the Law of the Sea, 'Settlement of Disputes Mechanism' (20 June 2017) at: http://www.un.org/Depts/los/settlement_of_disputes/choice_procedure.htm (last accessed 1 March 2018).

46 Article 287(5), UNCLOS.

47 L Dolliver M Nelson, 'Reflections on the 1982 Convention on the Law of the Sea', in David Freestone, Richard Barnes and David Ong (eds), *The Law of the Sea: Progress and Prospects* (Oxford University Press, Oxford: 2006) 28 at p. 35.

48 Part XV Article 297 2(b) and 3(b), and Annex V Section 2, UNCLOS.

These measures should therefore facilitate public consideration of issues such as maritime boundary delimitation.[49]

It is significant that UNCLOS refers to provisional arrangements, and therefore suggests an ultimate purpose of agreed boundaries rather than semi-permanent JDZs. The majority of JDZ agreements have been made where states have not been able to reach an agreement on the boundary.

UNCLOS therefore provides several alternative bases of dispute resolution, and it is strongly arguable that the current approaches would be fair to both parties. States may, however, consider that a decision by the ICJ or other dispute resolution process may result in the risk of a politically unacceptable loss of sovereign rights, whereas with a JDZ they may arrive at a negotiated settlement that does not include a determination on sovereign rights and is therefore acceptable to both states. The use of recent JDZs suggests that there may be a preference to negotiate directly towards a satisfactory sharing of resources from the disputed region.

2.3 *The Commission on the Limits of the Continental Shelf*

As illustrated in Figure 4, many of the maritime boundaries of the Arctic Ocean region will be substantially extended by the additional continental shelf permitted under UNCLOS. There have been several submissions by Arctic states to the CLCS, and further submissions are expected. The process for establishing the limits on the continental shelf by the CLCS is an essential part of Arctic boundary delimitation.

The CLCS was established under UNCLOS Article 76 and Annex II to analyse submissions from coastal states, and make recommendations on which to establish the limits of the continental shelf.[50] The coastal state is required to provide geographical data to support a continental shelf submission. The CLCS does not delimit maritime continental shelf boundaries between states with opposite or adjacent coasts. The CLCS may, however, make a recommendation on the continental shelf boundary without prejudice to maritime boundaries, where the other state agrees to this process.[51]

---

49 See Sienho Yee, 'Conciliation and the 1982 UN Convention on the Law of the Sea' (2013) 44(4) *Ocean Development and International Law* 321.

50 Annex II, Article 3, UNCLOS states the functions of the CLCS.

51 See for example the Australian submission to the CLCS made on a without-prejudice basis, Department of Foreign Affairs and Trade (Australia), 'Continental Shelf Submission of Australia, Executive Summary' AUS-DOC-ES (2004) at p. 6, at: http://www.un.org/Depts/los/clcs_new/submissions_files/aus04/Documents/aus_doc_es_web_delivery.pdf (last accessed 3 April 2018).

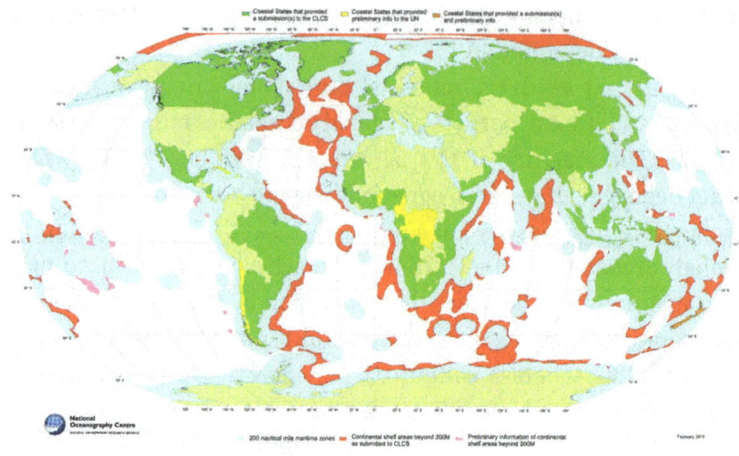

FIGURE 4 Continental shelf beyond 200 miles
SOURCE: NATIONAL OCEANOGRAPHY CENTRE (NOC), SOUTHAMPTON

The process of the CLCS is a technical evaluation of continental shelf submissions, rather than a legal evaluation or interpretation, and the members of the CLCS are experts in geology, geophysics or hydrology.[52] However, the members of the CLCS nevertheless have to engage in a level of legal interpretation, as the limits and definition of the continental shelf are contained in a legal instrument. The CLCS analyses the submissions by examining the data supplied by each state, including seabed features including the foot of slope feature, sediment thickness on the seabed floor, the 2500- metre-isobath depth line, submarine ridges, and submarine elevations. A significant issue arises in respect of 'submarine elevations,' because the continental shelf limit of 350 nautical miles in respect of submarine ridges does not apply to 'submarine elevations that are natural components of the continental margin, such as its plateaux, rises, caps, banks and spurs'.[53]

RR Churchill and AV Lowe commented that the continental shelf provisions in UNCLOS have been widely adopted in state practice declaring maritime boundaries adopting the '200 mile plus margin' limit based on UNCLOS

52 Donald R Rothwell, 'Issues and Strategies for Outer Continental Shelf Claims' (2008) 23 *International Journal of Marine and Coastal Law* 185 at p. 189.

53 Article 76(6), UNCLOS. Article 76(6) refers to submarine elevations 'that are natural components of the continental margin such as its plateaux, rises, caps, banks and spurs.'

Article 76,[54] including continental shelf declarations by Canada, Japan, Jamaica, Russia and South Africa.[55] Churchill and Lowe describe claims inconsistent with the Article 76 formula as scarce,[56] and concluded that '[i]t would be difficult to argue that any continental shelf claim consistent with the Article 76 formula was not compatible with customary international law.'[57] The ICJ considered the relationship between Article 76 and customary international law in the Territorial Dispute and Maritime Delimitation (Nicaragua v. Colombia) case.[58] The ICJ held that the definition of the continental shelf set out in Article 76, paragraph 1 forms part of customary international law.[59]

The CLCS faces several challenges in determining the continental shelf for states in the Arctic Ocean region. These issues include:

- The classification of submarine elevations and ridges, which is an essential issue for the Russian, Danish and Greenland government, and anticipated final Canadian continental shelf claim based on the Lomonosov Ridge;[60]
- The continental shelf may extend from adjacent coastal states where the maritime boundary is disputed. This issue may arise in the Arctic Ocean region between the United States and Russia in the Bering Sea,[61] or between the United States and Canada in the Beaufort Sea;[62]
- The continental shelf may lie between opposite coasts. This situation may arise in the Arctic Ocean region, where Canada or Denmark potentially

54 RR Churchill and AV Lowe, *The Law of the Sea* 3rd ed (Manchester University Press, Manchester: 1999) 149. Australia has also adopted the Article 76 OCS formula by adopting the recommendations of the CLCS; see *Seas and Submerged Lands (Limits of Continental Shelf) Proclamation 2012* (Australia), made pursuant to the *Seas and Submerged Lands Act 1973* (Australia).

55 Ibid.

56 Ibid., at p. 150. Churchill and Lowe commented that these claims were made by states including Ecuador, Chile and Iceland, and these declarations were protested by other states.

57 Ibid.

58 *Territorial Dispute and Maritime Delimitation* (Nicaragua v. Colombia) [2012] ICJ Rep 624.

59 *Territorial Dispute and Maritime Delimitation* (Nicaragua v. Colombia) [2012] ICJ Rep 624, para 118.

60 This issue relates to the classification of submarine elevations 'that are natural components of the continental margin such as its plateaux, rises, caps, banks and spurs.' and are therefore not limited to 350 nautical miles under Article 76(6).

61 The United States has used a median line basis, and Russia may potentially use a sector line.

62 Government of Canada, 'Beaufort Sea', at: http://publications.gc.ca/collection-r/lopbdp/bp/bp322-e.htm (last accessed 4 April 2018). Canada's use of the sector line is based on a historical treaty.

adopts a median line from the Russian coast and Russia uses a continental shelf approach extending beyond the median line;[63] and,

- The continental shelf may depend on the sovereignty of islands and whether the islands generate continental shelf under UNCLOS. Article 121 provides that islands generate EEZ and continental shelves, except if they are 'rocks which cannot sustain human habitation or economic life of their own'.[64] This issue may arise in the Arctic Ocean region between the United States and Russia in the Chukchi Sea.[65]

2.4 *The International Seabed Authority (ISBA) and the Arctic Ocean Region*

The ISBA was established under UNCLOS Part XI to develop the Area, which is defined as the sea-bed and ocean floor and subsoil beyond the limits of national jurisdiction.[66] UNCLOS declares the Area and its resources to be the common heritage of mankind,[67] and defines these resources to include all solid, liquid or gaseous mineral resources in the Area at or beneath the seabed.[68]

The Area regime was principally established for deep seabed mining of polymetallic nodules, polymetallic sulphides, and ferromanganese crusts located on the deep seabed. The regime would, however, also apply to oil and gas development, which may arise beyond the continental shelf in the longer term with related developments in technology.[69] Such activities would principally relate to the abyssal plain, which is generally defined as the seabed below

63 Martin Pratt, 'Maritime Jurisdiction and Boundaries in the Arctic Region' International Boundaries Research Unit (n.d.) at: http://www.dur.ac.uk/ibru/resources/arctic/ (last accessed 1 March 2018).

64 Article 121(3), UNCLOS.

65 United States Department of State, 'Bering Sea' (n.d.) at: http://www.state.gov/p/eur/rls/fs/128740.htm (last accessed 1 March 2018). The United States may consider that the Russian Herald Island does not affect the position of a median line or generate continental shelf and OCS zones.

66 Part XI, UNCLOS.

67 Article 136, UNCLOS.

68 Article 133, UNCLOS.

69 Though the related drilling was not in the Area, an example of deep-water drilling was the Transocean Ltd semi-submersible rig *Deepwater Horizon* drilling an oil and gas well for BP in the Gulf of Mexico off the United States, to 35,050 feet depth (more than six miles), while operating in 4,130 feet (1259 meters) of water; see *Scandinavian Oil and Gas Magazine* (3 September 2009) at: http://www.scandoil.com/moxie-bm2/news/transoceans-deepwater-horizon-drills-worlds-deepes.shtml (last accessed 1 March 2018).

2,000 meters water depth.[70] This depth should be considered in the light of the 2010 Deepwater Horizon offshore oil spill, where environmental measures failed at the Macondo well in the Gulf of Mexico at a water depth of 1,259 metres.[71] Environmental protection measures will be of extreme importance for any oil and gas development at the water depths in the Area.

The Part XI regime was substantially modified by the 1994 Agreement relating to the Implementation of Part XI of the United Nations Convention on the Law of the Sea (Implementation Agreement).[72] The Implementation Agreement was made in response to concerns expressed by United States and other states with the Part XI regime.[73] Changes were made to the ISBA decision-making process, the Finance Committee, the process of making licence applications to the ISBA, and the activities of the Enterprise.[74] Churchill and Lowe note that the Implementing Agreement abolished production ceilings and preferential treatment of the Enterprise, and that pioneer investors were approved in 1998.[75] Rothwell notes that since 1994 the Area regime has developed in important respects, including the finalisation in 2000 of the Regulations on Prospecting and Exploration for Polymetallic Nodules in the Area (Mining Code),[76] which address a range of administrative, contractual, legal,

70 Chris Park and Michael Allaby, *A Dictionary of Environment and Conservation* 3rd ed (Oxford University Press, Oxford: 2017) [online version].

71 The *Deepwater Horizon* rig was later involved in the Macondo oil spill in the Gulf of Mexico in 2010, indicating that offshore environmental protection technology currently lags significantly behind offshore drilling technology.

72 1994 Agreement relating to the Implementation of Part XI of the United Nations Convention on the Law of the Sea of 10 December 1982, 1994 *UNTS* 42 (1994 Implementation Agreement).

73 John Turner, 'Accession to the 1982 Law of the Sea Convention and Ratification of the 1994 Agreement Amending Part XI of the Law of the Sea Convention,' Testimony before the Senate Environment and Public Works Committee (23 March 2004), Senate Treaty Document 103–39; Senate Executive Report 108–10.

74 Bernard H. Oxman, 'The 1994 Agreement and the Convention' (1994) 88(4) *American Journal of International Law* 687, at pp. 689–695.

75 Churchill and Lowe (n. 54) at p. 251. The pioneer investors are the Government of India, the Institut Français pour l'exploitation de la Mer, Association Français pour l'étude et la Recherche des Nodules, Deep Ocean Resources Development Company, Yuzhmorgeologiya, China Ocean Mineral Research and Development Association, INTROCEANMETAL Joint Organisation.

76 International Seabed Authority, 'Decision of the Assembly relating to the regulations on prospecting and exploration for polymetallic nodules in the Area' (13 July 2000) UN Doc. ISBA/6/A/18 ('Mining Code').

and technical issues.[77] The Mining Code concerns polymetallic nodules, and a new code would be required for future oil and gas development. The development of the Mining Code and the approval of pioneer investors are significant, as this demonstrates the ISBA's capacity to develop and implement a regulatory regime. Following the changes under the Implementation Agreement, the ISBA's powers and responsibilities have essentially concerned administering the deep seabed mining regime, and the ISBA has signed 26 exploration contracts as of 2017.[78]

In relation to the potential for JDZs in the Arctic Ocean, the Area regime may have some similarities to JDZs to the extent that it potentially allows a form of multilateral resource sharing. There are important differences, however; in particular, activities in the Area need not involve states from the Arctic Ocean region. The Area regime is significant to at least two specific areas in the Arctic Ocean shown in the Arctic Boundary Map prepared by the International Boundaries Research Unit,[79] and one area in the western Norwegian Sea.[80] These regions are likely to be beyond current or potential Arctic state OCS submissions to the CLCS.[81]

2.5 *The Arctic Council*

The Arctic Council is an inter-governmental organisation originally established by Canada, Denmark, Finland, Iceland, Norway, Russia, Sweden and the United States at a meeting in Ottawa in 1996.[82] Membership of the Arctic Council includes these eight governments as voting members, together with

---

77 Donald R Rothwell, 'Building on the Strengths and Assessing the Challenges: The Role of Law of the Sea Institutions' (2004) 35 *Ocean Development and International Law* 131, at p. 136. These issues include the rights and obligations of prospectors and explorers, including the Enterprise, environmental protection, confidentiality, contracts with the ISBA, and dispute settlement.

78 Deep Seabed Minerals Contractors, International Seabed Authority, at: https://www.isa.org.jm/deep-seabed-minerals-contractors (last accessed 1 March 2018).

79 Pratt (n. 63).

80 The Area regime may also apply in the western Norwegian Sea between the Norwegian coast and Jan Mayen Island, subject to hydrographical surveys.

81 Alex G Oude Elferink and Donald R Rothwell, 'Challenges for Polar Maritime Delimitation and Jurisdiction: The Current Regime and its Prospects' in Alex G Oude Elferink and Donald R Rothwell (eds), *The Law of the Sea and Polar Maritime Delimitation and Jurisdiction* (Martinus Nijhoff, The Hague: 2001) 337, at p. 351.

82 Declaration on the Establishment of the Arctic Council, done in Ottawa on 19 September 1996, at http://arctic-council.org/article/about (last accessed 1 March 2018).

observer states,[83] indigenous community permanent participants,[84] and non-government observers.[85]

The five Arctic coastal states declared their support for the law of the sea to resolve boundary issues in the Ilulissat Declaration in 2008. The Declaration stated that Arctic Council members 'remain committed to this legal framework and to the orderly settlement of any possible overlapping claims.'[86] Accordingly, although the Arctic Council is a forum for promoting cooperation in certain measures discussed below for the Arctic Ocean region, the members do not propose to establish a separate legal regime, such as a regime independent of the dispute resolution provisions of UNCLOS, for the resolution of maritime boundaries and competing offshore claims.

The Arctic Council released the Arctic Offshore Oil and Gas Guidelines (AOOGG) in 2009.[87] The guidelines include environmental impact statements, environmental monitoring, safety and environmental management, operating practices, emergencies, decommissioning, and site clearance. The Arctic Council released the related Arctic Offshore Oil and Gas Guidelines: Systems Safety

83 The observer states, as at April 2018, are France, Germany, Italy, Japan, the Netherlands, China, Poland, India, Korea, Singapore, Spain, Switzerland and the United Kingdom.

84 The Declaration on the Establishment of the Arctic Council (n. 82) stated that:

"The purpose of the Arctic Council is to promote cooperation, coordination and interaction among the Arctic States, with the involvement of the Arctic indigenous communities and other Arctic inhabitants on common Arctic issues, in particular issues of sustainable development and environmental protection in the Arctic."

The Russian government suspended the Russian Association of Indigenous People of the North ('RAIPON') which is a Permanent Participant of the Arctic Council from 1 November 2011 to 20 April 2012. 'RAIPON's Activities Suspended', Arctic Council Indigenous Peoples Secretariat (17 November 2012) at: http://www.arcticpeoples.org (last accessed 1 March 2018). RAIPON received approval to renew its activities in 2013, however, following Russian Federal Ministry of Justice approval of amendments in the organisation's statutes.

85 The Arctic Council previously included ad-hoc participants which were required to request permission for their presence at each individual meeting. The ad-hoc participants requested full observer status in 2009, and the Arctic Council confirmed these states as permanent observers in 2013.

86 (2009) 48 *ILM* 382 (Ilulissat Declaration). The representatives of the Canadian, Denmark, Norway, Russian Federation and United States governments, at a meeting at Ilulissat in Greenland in May 2008, declared that:

"Notably, the law of the sea provides for important rights and obligations concerning the delineation of the outer limits of the continental shelf, the protection of the marine environment, including ice-covered areas, freedom of navigation, marine scientific research, and other uses of the sea. We remain committed to this legal framework and to the orderly settlement of any possible overlapping claims."

87 Arctic Council, 'Arctic Offshore Oil and Gas Guidelines, 2009, at: https://oaarchive.arctic-council.org/handle/11374/63 (last accessed 3 April 2018).

Management and Safety Culture in 2015, which provides tools and approaches for reducing the threat of catastrophic effects of major oil and gas-related accidents, such as the 2010 Deepwater Horizon disaster.[88]

The Agreement on Cooperation on Marine Oil Pollution, Preparedness and Response in the Arctic was concluded in May 2013.[89] The Agreement introduces a binding regime for Arctic Marine Oil Pollution Preparedness and Response (MOPPR).[90] MOPPR is the Arctic regional implementation of the OPRC Convention.[91] The Agreement set out requirements for national systems for pollution preparedness and response, notification to other parties of oil pollution incidents, monitoring Arctic maritime areas for possible oil pollution incidents, and coordination of joint response operations.[92]

3 Maritime Disputes in the Arctic and Areas Suitable for JDZs

3.1 *Boundary Claims and Arctic State Submissions to the CLCS*

The following review analyses the maritime boundaries and related continental shelf claims of states in the Arctic Ocean, commencing with the United States, and moving in an easterly direction about the North Pole for the states with Arctic coastlines. One threshold issue is the extent to which Arctic states have accepted dispute resolution procedures under UNCLOS.[93] No Arctic state has accepted compulsory arbitration under UNCLOS in relation to maritime boundary delimitation provided under UNCLOS Article 298 and, as noted above, the United States is not a party to UNCLOS.

88 Arctic Council, 'Arctic Offshore Oil and Gas Guidelines. Systems Safety Management and Safety Culture. Avoiding Major Disasters in Arctic Offshore Oil and Gas Operations', at: https://oaarchive.arctic-council.org/handle/11374/418 (last accessed 1 March 2018).

89 2013 Agreement on Cooperation on Marine Oil Pollution, Preparedness and Response in the Arctic (not yet in force) at: https://oaarchive.arctic-council.org/handle/11374/529 (last accessed 1 March 2018) (Arctic MOPPR).

90 Arctic Council, Senior Arctic Officials (SAO) Report to Ministers, Nuuk, Greenland (May 2011) 4.

91 1990 International Convention on Oil Pollution Preparedness, Response and Cooperation, 1891 *UNTS* 51 (OPRC Convention).

92 Arctic Council, Protection of the Arctic Marine Environment Working Group, The Arctic Ocean Review Project, Phase II Report 2011–2013, at: http://www.arctic-council.org/index.php/en/oceans/arctic-ocean-review/396-phase-ii-of-the-arctic-ocean-review-project (last accessed 1 March 2018).

93 United Nations Division for Ocean Affairs and the Law of the Sea, 'Settlement of Disputes Mechanism' (n.d.), at: http://www.un.org/Depts/los/settlement_of_disputes/choice_procedure.htm (last accessed 1 March 2018).

The choices made by states with Arctic claims and dispute resolution declarations on UNCLOS dispute resolution provisions are summarised in Table 1.

A significant issue in delimitation is the status of continental shelf submissions to the CLCS. These submissions establish the outer limits of state rights, and the potential overlapping claims of these increased areas of state rights may be included in potential JDZs in these regions. Submissions

TABLE 1 Arctic state UNCLOS dispute resolution declarations

	ITLOS	**ICJ**	**Arbitration Annex VII**	**Special Arbitration annex VIII**	**Exception declared under UNCLOS Section 298 type of dispute – Boundary delimitation is (a)**
United States	NR-UNCLOS	N/A	N/A	N/A	N/A
Canada	1	–	1	–	1(a), (b) and (c)
Denmark	–	1	Not accepted for any 298 dispute	–	Declared for all categories
Norway	–	1	–	–	Declared for all categories
Iceland	NCF	NCF	NCF	NCF	Interpretation of Article 83 submitted to conciliation
Russia	Prompt release cases	–	1	Fisheries, marine environment, scientific research and navigation	1(a), (b) and (c)

NR-UNCLOS – the state has not ratified UNCLOS; NCF – no choice of forum made and expected submissions to the CLCS relating to the Arctic Ocean region are as follows:[94]

TABLE 2 Arctic state submissions to the CLCS

Country	Ratified UNCLOS[a]	Arctic Ocean CLCS Submission Lodged, Due[b] or Preliminary Information[c]	CLCS Recommendation	Arctic Ocean recommendation adopted by State Legislation
Canada	7 November 2003	Preliminary Submission in respect of the Arctic on 6 December 2013 provided that its final submission would be submitted at a later date in accordance with SPLOS/183.		
Denmark – (Greenland)	16 November 2004, entered into force 16 December 2004	15 December 2014		
Norway	24 June 1996, entered into force 24 July 1996	27 November 2006	27 March 2009	
Russia	12 March 1997	20 December 2001	14 June 2002.[d] further submission requested by the CLCS, partial revised submission made on 3 August 2015	

94 The deadline for outer continental shelf submissions for states such as Canada and Denmark, which did not ratify UNCLOS prior to 13 May 1999, is determined under Article 308(2), UNCLOS.

TABLE 2 Arctic state submissions to the CLCS (*cont.*)

Country	Ratified UNCLOS[a]	Arctic Ocean CLCS Submission Lodged, Due[b] or Preliminary Information[c]	CLCS Recommendation	Arctic Ocean recommendation adopted by State Legislation
United States	UNCLOS not yet acceded to			

a United Nations Division for Ocean Affairs and the Law of the Sea, 'Chronological Lists of Ratifications of, Accessions and Successions to the Convention and Related Agreements' (3 April 2018) at: http://www.un.org/Depts/los/reference_files/chronological_lists_of_ratifications.htm (last accessed 4 April 2018).

b United Nations Division for Ocean Affairs and the Law of the Sea (n.d.) at: http://www.un.org/Depts/los/clcs_new/clcs_home.htm (last accessed 4 April 2018).

c United Nations Division for Ocean Affairs and the Law of the Sea, 'Preliminary information indicative of the outer limits of the continental shelf beyond 200 nautical miles' (8 December 2017) at: http://www.un.org/Depts/los/clcs_new/commission_preliminary.htm (last accessed 4 April 2018).

d United Nations Commission on the Limits of the Continental Shelf, 'Statement by the Chairman of the Commission on the Limits of the Continental Shelf on the progress of work in the Commission' (24-28 June 2002) UN Doc. CLCS/34, 33.

Significant developments include the agreement between Norway and Russia on a maritime boundary in the Barents Sea in 2010,[95] and an agreement, still to be formalised by a treaty, between Canada and Denmark on the maritime boundary in the Lincoln Sea in 2012.[96] The most significant anticipated development is likely to be the CLCS recommendation on the revised Russian submission for the claimed continental shelf. Other significant developments are the Danish and Greenland government continental shelf submission made on 15 December 2014, the anticipated final continental shelf submissions for Canada and the potential for a United States continental shelf submission in

95 2010 Treaty Between the Kingdom of Norway and the Russian Federation Concerning Maritime Delimitation and Cooperation in the Barents Sea and the Arctic Ocean, 2791 *UNTS* I-49095, Registration No 49095, Norwegian Government, Office of the Prime Minister.

96 Government of Canada, Foreign Affairs and International Trade Canada, 'Canada and Kingdom of Denmark Reach Tentative Agreement on Lincoln Sea Boundary' (Press Release, 28 November 2012) at: http://www.international.gc.ca/media/aff/news-communiques/2012/11/28a.aspx?view=d (last accessed 4 April 2018).

respect of the Chukchi Sea region in the event the United States accedes to UNCLOS.

Canada stated in its 2013 partial submission in relation to the Atlantic Ocean that its submission in relation to the Arctic would be submitted at a later date in accordance with Article 4 of Annex II of UNCLOS and the eighteenth Meeting of States Parties to the Law of the Sea (SPLOS/183).[97] Canada then lodged the Preliminary Information concerning the outer limits of the continental shelf of Canada in the Arctic Ocean on 6 December 2013.[98] The International Boundaries Research Unit (IBRU) summarised current and potential continental shelf claims in the Arctic Ocean region in 2008 with several more recent updates.[99]

The most significant geographical features affecting the current Russian continental shelf submission and Danish (Greenland) continental shelf submissions, and the anticipated Canadian Arctic submission, are the Lomonosov and Alpha/Mendeleev Ridges.[100] The Ridges may potentially support the continental shelves of the respective states extending beyond 350 nautical miles. The extent of the potential Russian, Canadian and Danish continental shelf relating to the Lomonosov and Alpha/Mendeleev Ridges will be determined under the more specific provisions for 'oceanic ridges', 'submarine ridges', and 'submarine elevations':

- If the ridges are 'oceanic ridges', they are excluded from the continental margin under Article 76(3), and so these features do not support the continental shelf. 'Oceanic ridges' are not defined in UNCLOS;
- If the ridges are 'submarine ridges', the continental shelf is limited to 350 nautical miles under Article 76(6); and
- If the Lomonosov and Mendeleev Ridges are 'submarine elevations that are natural components of the continental margin', the continental shelf is limited to the 2500 meter isobath line plus 100 nautical miles, under Article

97 Government of Canada, 'Partial Submission of Canada to the Commission on the Limits of the Continental Shelf regarding its continental shelf in the Atlantic Ocean, Executive Summary' (2013) 3 http://www.un.org/depts/los/clcs_new/submissions_files/can70_13/es_can_en.pdf (last accessed 3 April 2018).

98 Government of Canada, 'Preliminary Information concerning the outer limits of the continental shelf of Canada in the Arctic Ocean' (6 December 2013) at: http://www.un.org/depts/los/clcs_new/submissions_files/preliminary/can_pi_en.pdf (last accessed 1 March 2018). The filing of the preliminary information satisfied the time period in Article 4 of Annex II of the Convention, read in conjunction with decision SPLOS/183 adopted at the eighteenth meeting of States Parties to the Convention.

99 Pratt (n. 63).

100 The Alpha Ridge extends from the Canadian Arctic coast towards the Mendeleev Ridge extending to the Russian coast.

76(6). These limits may exceed 350 nautical miles. 'Submarine elevations' are not defined in UNCLOS.

The difficulty in interpretation for the CLCS is generally in classifying undersea structures between these categories. The United States has commented on the Lomonosov Ridge,[101] and the Mendeleev Ridge,[102] and concluded they were not related to the continental margins.[103]

3.2 *State Boundary Claims and Agreements*

The following analysis of Arctic maritime boundaries is based in part on research by IBRU: 'Maritime jurisdictions and boundaries in the Arctic region', originally published in 2008 with recent updates illustrated in Figure 5.[104] Sovereignty over land and island features in the Arctic region is generally now agreed.[105] There have, however, been previous disputes as to sovereignty as discussed below. The status of land claims in the Arctic is also not static. In particular, there is an expectation of future full independence of Greenland from Denmark, which will alter governance regimes relating to Greenland's potential offshore oil and gas resources.

3.2.1 United States/Russia (Bering Sea and Chukchi Sea)

The Bering Sea boundary region between the United States and Russia is illustrated in Figure 6. The United States and Russia have an unresolved maritime boundary in the Bering and Chukchi Seas extending to the Arctic Ocean.[106] The United States and Russia signed the Agreement on the Maritime Boundary on

---

101 United States of America, 'Notification Regarding the Submission made by the Russian Federation to the Commission on the Limits of the Continental Shelf', Ref. No. CLCS.01.2001.LOS/USA (18 March 2002) 3. The United States commented as follows: "The Ridge is a freestanding feature in the deep, oceanic part of the Arctic Ocean Basin, and not a natural component at the continental margins at either Russia or any other State."

102 Ibid. The United States commented as follows: "The Alpha-Mendeleev Ridge System is the surface expression of a single continuous geologic feature that formed on oceanic crust at the Arctic Ocean basin by volcanism over a 'hot spot'."

103 Ibid. The United States concluded: "Both aeromagnetic and bathymetric data show that the ridges extend entirely across the Arctic Ocean, which characteristic aeromagnetic expression ends at the continental margins at both ends and is absent from adjacent continental shelves."

104 Pratt (n. 63).

105 The exception is the dispute between Denmark and Canada concerning Hans Island discussed below.

106 United States Department of State, 'Status of Wrangel and Other Arctic Islands', Fact Sheet, Bureau of European and Eurasian Affairs, Washington (20 May 2003) at: https://2001–2009.state.gov/p/eur/rls/fs/20922.htm (last accessed 4 April 2018).

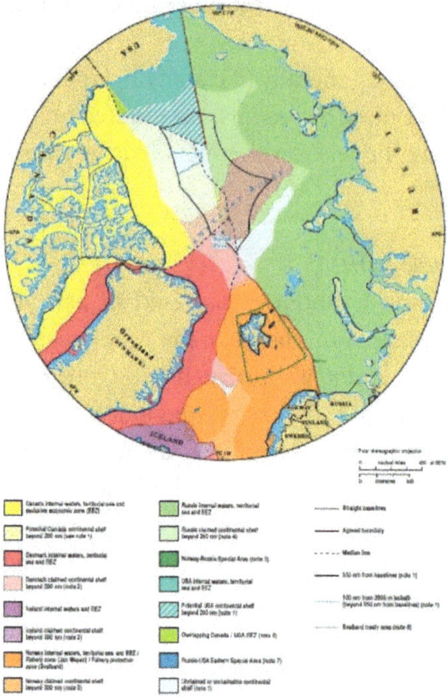

FIGURE 5
Arctic maritime boundaries
SOURCE: IBRU, DURHAM UNIVERSITY, UK HTTPS://WWW.DUR.AC.UK/IBRU/RESOURCES/ARCTIC/

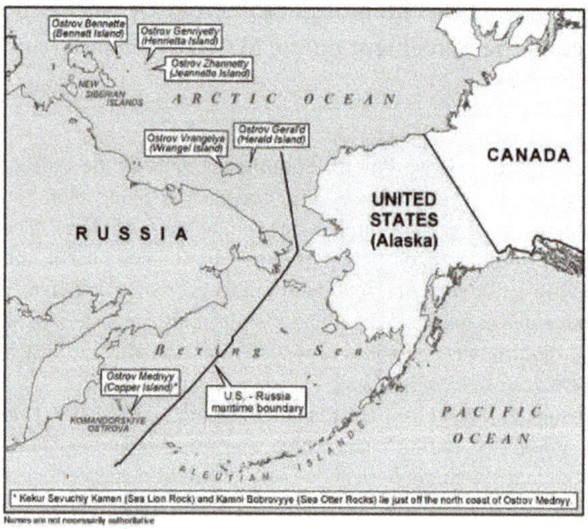

FIGURE 6
Bering sea maritime boundary
SOURCE: UNITED STATES DEPARTMENT OF STATE

1 June 1990 ('1990 Agreement'),[107] to delimit the boundary from the Bering Sea to the Arctic Ocean. The Soviet Union and successor Russian governments have not, however, ratified the Agreement.[108] In an exchange of diplomatic notes in 1991 and 1992, the two states agreed to apply the Agreement provisionally.[109] The Russian Assembly rejected a bill to approve the continued application of the 1990 Agreement in 1997.[110]

The circumstances of the 1990 Agreement included the prior United States purchase of substantial territories from the Russian Empire in 1867[111] ('Alaska Purchase'),[112] including the definition of the western boundary.[113] This was interpreted by the Soviet Union as establishing the boundary based on connecting 'rhumb lines', which cross meridian lines at the same angle,[114] and by the United States as arcs of great circles.[115] The result was an area of overlapping claims in the Bering Sea of approximately 21,000 square nautical miles. Verville describes the outcome of the 1990 Agreement as allowing to each country one half of the disputed areas of the Bering Sea.[116]

---

107 1990 Agreement between the United States of America and the Union of Soviet Socialist Republics on the Maritime Boundary (not yet in force at 28 February 2018) United States Department of State, at: http://www.state.gov/documents/organization/125431.pdf (last accessed 1 March 2018) (United States/Russia 1990 Agreement).

108 United States ratification was made on 16 September 1991.

109 Alex G Oude Elferink, 'Arctic Maritime Delimitations: The Preponderance of Similarities with Other Regions' in Alex G Oude Elferink and Donald R Rothwell (eds), *The Law of the Sea and Polar Maritime Delimitation and Jurisdiction* (Martinus Nijhoff, The Hague: 2001) 179, at p. 183.

110 United States Department of State (n. 110). The report stated that Russia advised the United States on 13 January 1992 that it 'continues to perform the rights and fulfil the obligations flowing from the international agreements' signed by the Soviet Union.

111 Elizabeth G Verville, 'United States – Soviet Union, Report Number 1–6', in Jonathan I Charney and Lewis M Alexander (eds), *International Maritime Boundaries* Vol 1 (Martinus Nijhoff, Dordrecht/Boston: 1993) 447.

112 1867 Treaty concerning the Cession of the Russian Possessions in North America by his Majesty the Emperor of all the Russias to the United States of America, 15 *Stat* 539, (Alaska Purchase).

113 Article 1, Alaska Purchase. This defined the western boundary extending from midway between what are now the Diomede Islands, generally extending southwest through the Bering Sea, between the midpoints of specified islands and land territories, and intersections of specific lines of longitude.

114 The rhumb line is the line crossing all meridians of longitude at the same angle.

115 The arc of the great circle is a part of a circle drawn on the earth's surface, with the centre at the centre of the earth.

116 Verville (n. 115) at p. 451. The 1990 Agreement is of particular interest as it was negotiated at a time of adversarial political relations between the two countries.

The United States received approximately 70 per cent of the Bering Sea under the 1990 Agreement. The Agreement provided for small 'special areas', to transfer EEZ rights from the state with a coast within 200 nautical miles to the state with a more distant coast, to prevent the fishery resources of these areas being subject to neither state's jurisdiction.[117] The transfer of rights to the United States were the 'eastern special areas' relating to Wrangel Island, Cape Navarin, and the Medny Island regions, and transfer of rights to Russia for the 'western special area' relating to the Attu Island region. This is similar to the 'special area' under the Norway/Russia Barents Sea Treaty.[118]

3.2.2 United States Arctic Coast – Alaska

United States sovereignty over Alaska is based upon acquisition of Russian rights to Alaska in the 1867 Treaty.[119] No state contests United States sovereignty over the land area; however, there are related maritime boundary disputes with Canada, including the Beaufort Sea discussed below. The United States declared an EEZ extending out to 200 nautical miles from the baselines, on a basis which is consistent with UNCLOS.[120] The United States has also declared a continental shelf, based on the 1958 Convention on the Continental Shelf.[121] This claim does not extend beyond 200 nautical miles.[122] If the United States accedes to UNCLOS, it will then have 10 years to make a continental shelf claim

117 Article 3, United States/Russia 1990 Agreement; and United States, Department of State, 'Message From The President Of The United States Transmitting the Agreement Between The United States Of America And The Union of Soviet Socialist Republics on the Maritime Boundary, with Annex, Signed at Washington, June 1, 1990,' vii and ix, at: http://www.state.gov/documents/organization/125431.pdf (last accessed 4 April 2018).

118 2010 Treaty Between the Kingdom of Norway and the Russian Federation Concerning Maritime Delimitation and Cooperation in the Barents Sea and the Arctic Ocean, 2791 *UNTS* I-49095.

119 1867 Treaty concerning the Cession of the Russian Possessions in North America by his Majesty the Emperor of all the Russias to the United States of America, 15 Stat 539, (*Alaska Treaty*). The purchase price was USD 7.2 million. There was a political advantage to Russia in preventing Great Britain from occupying Alaska, and restricting potential expansion of Great Britain's colony of British Columbia established in 1858.

120 *United States Presidential Proclamation* 5030 (10 March 1983) 3 C.F.R. 22; *Magnuson Act of 1950, Magnuson Act of 1950*, 50 USC §191 (1950) (definition of EEZ); United States Federal Register, 60 F.R. 43825 (23 August1995) (public notice of the limits of the U.S. EEZ).

121 1958 Convention on the Continental Shelf, 499 *UNTS* 312. The Convention defined the continental shelf based on exploitability, rather than a geographical limit.

122 United States Presidential Proclamation 2667 (28 September 1945) 3 CFR 67; *Outer Continental Shelf Lands Act of 1953*, 43 USC § 1331(a) (2001).

beyond 200 nautical miles, which may extend from the north coast of Alaska into the Arctic Ocean.[123]

The United States' right to a 200-nautical-mile continental shelf would be consistent with the Convention on the Continental Shelf,[124] if this claim met the Convention's criteria, which depends on depth and exploitability of the resources of the continental shelf. The United States government has considered the potential adoption of UNCLOS, including implementing several aspects of UNCLOS in domestic legislation.[125] The United States *Fishery Conservation and Management Act of 1976*,[126] and the *Deep Seabed Hard Mineral Resources Act*,[127] have been described by Marjorie Ann Browne as 'interim measures prior to entry into force of a Law of the Sea.'[128]

The process of submission to the CLCS to obtain a recommendation on the outer limits of the continental shelf beyond 200 nautical miles does not mean that the United States is not entitled to a continental shelf. This is because continental shelf rights are inherent to states under customary international law. The inability to use the procedure involving the CLCS has implications, however, for the acceptance of the outer limits by other states and the international community more generally.[129]

The potential United States continental shelf region relating to the Chukchi plateau underwater peninsula, north of the Alaskan coast and adjacent to Russia, is known as the 'Chukchi Cap'. Marc Benitah considered that this claim would be based on Article 76(6) of UNCLOS, relating to 'submarine elevations that are natural components of the continental margin.'[130] The

123 The potential United States continental shelf would extend from the north-western Alaskan coast in the Chukchi Sea, northwards into the Arctic Ocean, and the Beaufort Sea area from the north-eastern Alaskan coast, adjacent to Canada northwards to the Arctic Ocean.

124 Article 1, Convention on the Continental Shelf.

125 United States Department of State, 'Law of the Sea Convention Letters of Transmittal and Submittal and Commentary', Dispatch Volume 6, Supplement Number 1 (February 1995) at: http://dosfan.lib.uic.edu/ERC/briefing/dispatch/1995/html/Dispatchv6Sup1.html (last accessed 4 April 2018).

126 *Fishery Conservation and Management Act of 1976*, 16 § USC 1801–1882 (1996) (also known as the *Magnuson – Stevens Act*).

127 *Deep Seabed Hard Mineral Resources Act*, 30 USC § 1401 (1980).

128 Marjorie Ann Browne, 'The Law of the Sea Convention and U.S. Policy', *CRS Issue Brief for Congress* (10 February 2005) 11, at: http://www.fas.org/sgp/crs/row/IB95010.pdf (last accessed 1 March 2018).

129 Annex II, Article 4, UNCLOS.

130 Marc Benitah, 'Russia's Claim in the Arctic and the Vexing Issue of Ridges in UNCLOS' (2007) *American Society of International Law ASIL Insight* 11, at: http://www.asil.org/insights/2007/11/insights071108.html (last accessed 4 April 2018).

recommendation from the President to the United States Senate for the adoption of UNCLOS in 1994 stated that the Chukchi Cap was not considered a ridge, but rather a submarine elevation that was a natural component of the continental margin, therefore allowing a continental shelf claim exceeding 350 nautical miles from the Alaskan coast.[131] Benitah commented that this category of claim under UNCLOS may also be used in the Russian claim relating to the Lomonosov and Mendeleev ridges, as discussed below. The extent of any potential overlaps between a future United States continental shelf submission, and submission by the Russian, Danish, and Greenland governments, and a future Canadian submission, will not be known until the submissions are finalised, and the related recommendations are made by the CLCS. The region has potential for substantial reserves of oil and gas, and Shell has conducted exploratory drilling in the Chukchi and Beaufort seas north of the Alaskan coast.[132]

3.2.3 United States/Canada – Beaufort Sea

The Beaufort Sea maritime boundary region between the United States and Canada is illustrated in Figure 7. Canada proclaimed a baseline claim in the Arctic region in 1985, in general from the boundary with the United States to the entrance to the Hudson Strait.[133] There is a dispute with the United States in relation to an area of the EEZ and continental shelf of about 6,250 square miles in relation to the Beaufort Sea, where the Canadian claim extends north from the land boundary, whereas the United States claim is based on equidistance.[134] There is also a potentially larger dispute as to the continental shelf boundaries; however, the potential boundary dispute has yet to fully crystallise, as Canada made only a preliminary submission without full details to the CLCS on 6 December 2013, and the United States, not being a party to UNCLOS, has made no submission to the CLCS.

---

131 William Jefferson Clinton, 'Message from the President of the United States and Commentary Accompanying the United Nations Convention on the Law of the Sea and the Agreement Relating to the Implementation of Part XI Upon their Transmittal to the United States Senate for its Advice and Consent' (1994) *Georgetown International Environmental Law Review* 7, at p. 147.

132 Shell Global, 'Shell Updates on Alaska Exploration' (28 September 2015) at: https://www.shell.com/media/news-and-media-releases/2015/shell-updates-on-alaska-exploration.html (last accessed 2 March 2018). There was a suspension of these activities in 2013 owing to economic and environmental concerns.

133 Territorial Sea Geographic Coordinates (Area 7) Order of 10 September 1985, Canada Gazette, Part II (2 October 1985).

134 Government of Canada, 'The Law of the Sea Convention' BP-322E, at: http://publications.gc.ca/Collection-R/LoPBdP/BP/bp322-e.htm#c. The Beaufort Sea Dispute(txt) (last accessed 3 April 2018).

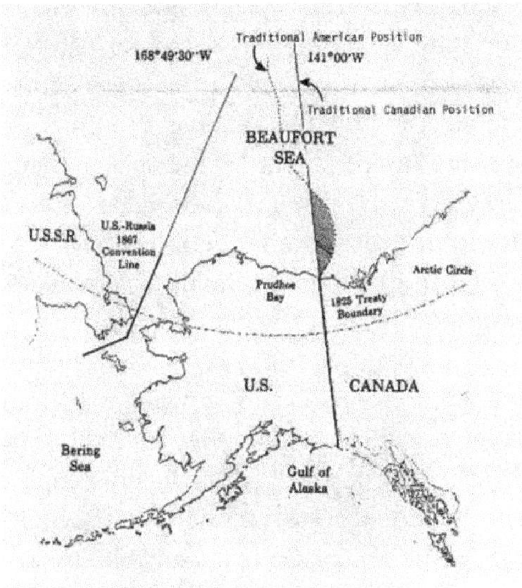

FIGURE 7
Beaufort sea maritime boundary region
SOURCE: KARIN L. LAWSON, 'DELIMITING CONTINENTAL SHELF BOUNDARIES IN THE ARCTIC: THE UNITED STATES—CANADA BEAUFORT SEA BOUNDARY' (1981) 22 VIRGINIA JOURNAL OF INTERNATIONAL LAW 222.

David Gray has commented that the basis for the Canadian boundary claim is a meridian line at 141 degrees of latitude, based on the 1825 Convention between Great Britain and Russia.[135] The Convention defined the boundary as 141 degrees of latitude, 'in its prolongation as far as the frozen ocean.'[136] The United States claim is based on the adoption of Russian rights under the agreement for the purchase of Alaska in 1867,[137] and the claim that the related boundary should be based on equidistance. Canada subsequently has adopted Great Britain's rights. The interpretation is based on the original French language of the treaty, and the dispute may need future resolution before the boundary can be agreed.[138]

Canada granted two exploration leases in the 1980s; however, these leases are currently inactive owing to work prohibition orders. The United States has included the overlapping claim area in lease sales since 1982, including related lease sales in 2007; however, these leases do not permit drilling until the dispute

135 1825 Convention between Great Britain and Russia concerning the limits of their Respective Possessions on the North-West Coast of America and the Navigation of the Pacific Ocean, 75 *CTS* 95.

136 David Gray, 'Canada's Unresolved Maritime Boundaries' (1997) *IBRU Boundary and Security Bulletin* 61.

137 1867 Convention between the United States of America and His Majesty the Emperor of Russia, for the Cession of the Russian Possessions in North America to the United States, 134 *CTS* 331.

138 Gray (n. 140) at p. 63.

is resolved.[139] A shared access approach discussed in 1977 may potentially have an established boundary, where each state would then have had the right of purchase to half the volume of hydrocarbons produced in the other state's part of the shared zone.[140] McDorman has commented that the 'Beaufort Sea boundary dispute area has long been seen as a candidate for the development of some type of hydrocarbon joint development regime.'[141] Existing leases also add a complexity to negotiations for joint hydrocarbon development agreements, and there have not been significant discussions of joint development since that date. This may potentially change owing to the increasing interest in oil and gas resources in the region.

Canada may also have an internal issue in relation to any new maritime boundary,[142] as the currently claimed boundary was used to set out rights and obligations between the Canadian government and the Inuvialuit peoples under the Inuvialuit Final Agreement.[143] One suggested solution was based on Canadian management of the region, under a joint development agreement, with a portion of the related profits paid to the United States.[144]

The Beaufort Sea continental shelf dispute may be considered in the broader context of a potential dispute over future United States and Canadian continental shelf claims. Baker and Byers argued that the United States approach, based on equidistance, may reduce the potential United States continental shelf area, owing to the proximity of Banks and Prince Patrick islands in the Canadian Northwest Territories, and that the use of equidistance beyond 200 nautical miles would favour the potential Canadian continental shelf.[145] The United States' response to the potential Canadian submission may be to present a 'no objection' note to the CLCS, on the basis that the CLCS consideration should be made without prejudice to a future boundary agreement.[146]

---

139 Ted L McDorman, *Salt Water Neighbors – International Ocean Relations between the United States and Canada* (Oxford University Press, New York/Oxford: 2009) 181.

140 Ibid., at p. 189. This arrangement would have enabled the retention of the two national regimes regulating oil and gas development.

141 Ibid., at p. 188.

142 James S Baker and Michael Byers, 'Crossed Lines: The Curious Case of the Beaufort Sea Maritime Boundary Dispute' (2012) 43(1) *Ocean Development and International Law* 70, at p. 78.

143 1984 Agreement between the Committee for Original Peoples' Entitlement, representing the Inuvialuit of the Inuvialuit Settlement Region and the Government of Canada, at: http://www.irc.inuvialuit.com/inuvialuit-final-agreement (last accessed 4 April 2018) (Inuvialuit Final Agreement).

144 Michael Byers, *International Law and the Arctic* (Cambridge University Press, Cambridge: 2013) 89.

145 Baker and Byers (n. 146) at p. 78.

146 Ibid., at p. 85.

In relation to oil and gas reserves, Canada has been conducting oil and gas activities and is extending these activities further offshore. Both Canada[147] and the United States[148] have granted conflicting offshore exploration leases in the disputed zone.

3.2.4 Canadian Arctic Coast – Lomonosov and Alpha Ridges

The northern coastline of Canada is defined under the Canadian baseline claim in the Arctic region in 1985, and follows the outer boundary of Canada's Arctic islands including Banks, Ellesmere and Baffin Islands.[149] The baselines were declared in 1985 with the purpose of ensuring Canadian national security with respect to the predicted increase in foreign commercial and military navigation.[150] The Canadian declaration followed the voyage of the United States Coast Guard icebreaker USCGC *Polar Sea* through the Northwest Passage earlier in that year.

Canada ratified UNCLOS in 2003, and its continental shelf submission was originally required to be lodged with the CLCS by 6 December 2013.[151] Canada stated in its 2013 partial submission in relation to the Atlantic Ocean that its submission in relation to the Arctic would be submitted at a later date in accordance with Article 4 of Annex II of UNCLOS and the eighteenth Meeting of States Parties to the Law of the Sea (SPLOS/183).[152] Canada then lodged the Preliminary Information concerning the outer limits of the continental shelf of Canada in the Arctic Ocean on 6 December 2013.[153] The Preliminary

147 Government of Canada, Oil and Gas Dispositions https://www.aadnc-aandc.gc.ca/dam/dam-inter-hq-nog/staging/texte-text/le_mp_bsmd_pg_1371579383933_eng.pdf (last accessed 3 April 2018).

148 National Oceanic and Atmospheric Administration (United States of America), 'Federal and State Offshore Oil & Gas Leases, Beaufort & Chukchi Seas' (n.d.) at: www.nmfs.noaa.gov/pr/pdfs/permits/openwater/map.pdf (last accessed 4 April 2018).

149 Territorial Sea Geographic Coordinates (Area 7) Order of 10 September 1985, Canada Gazette, Part II (2 October 1985).

150 Tullio Scovazzi, 'The Baseline of the Territorial Sea: The Practice of Arctic States', in Alex G Oude Elferink and Donald R Rothwell (eds) *The Law of the Sea and Polar Maritime Delimitation and Jurisdiction* (Martinus Nijhoff, The Hague: 2001) 69, at p. 76.

151 Government of Canada, Fisheries and Oceans Canada, 'Canada's Submission to the Commission on the Limits of the Continental Shelf Under the United Nations Convention on the Law of the Sea (The 'Continental Shelf Program')' (22 September 2009) at: http://www.dfo-mpo.gc.ca/ae-ve/evaluations/09-10/6b060-eng.htm (last accessed 4 April 2018).

152 Ibid., and Government of Canada (n. 101).

153 'Preliminary Information concerning the outer limits of the continental shelf of Canada in the Arctic Ocean' (6 December 2013) at: http://www.un.org/depts/los/clcs_new/commission_preliminary.htm (last accessed 4 April 2018). The filing of the preliminary information satisfied the time period in Article 4, Annex II, UNCLOS, read in conjunction with decision SPLOS/183 adopted at the eighteenth meeting of States Parties to UNCLOS.

Information is significant as it provides for a submission based on the Alpha and Lomonosov Ridges.[154]

In relation to the expected final submission, Canada has been surveying the Alpha Ridge,[155] extending from the north coast of Ellesmere Island northwest into the Arctic Ocean, and the Lomonosov Ridge extending from Ellesmere Island and Greenland north into the Arctic Ocean.[156] The Canadian continental shelf submission relating to the Lomonosov and Alpha Ridges overlaps the Russian claim extending from the Russian coast to the North Pole.[157] The extent of an overlap, if any, between a full Canadian continental shelf submission, and the continental shelf submission of the Danish and Greenland governments made in December 2014, will not be known until the full Canadian submission, and the related recommendations by the CLCS, are made.

The issue may be determined by whether there is sufficient scientific evidence that the Lomonosov and Alpha Ridges are natural prolongations of the Canadian continental margin. The ridges extend across the North Pole between the American and Asian continents, and this suggests that they are not natural prolongations of only one continental margin; however, the final determination must be made by the CLCS. If the final Canadian submission extends beyond the North Pole to overlap the Russian submission, then the CLCS may make recommendations without prejudice to the resulting boundary dispute. There are at present no indications whether the Canadian submission will extend beyond the North Pole; however, the Danish and Greenland government submission did extend beyond the North Pole.

3.2.5 Canada/Denmark (Greenland) – Lincoln Sea

The major portion of the maritime boundary between Canada and Denmark in the Lincoln Sea region was agreed between the two states in 1973.[158] The

154 Ibid. The Preliminary Information stated: "The continental margin of Canada in the Arctic Ocean is part of a morphologically continuous continental margin around the Canada Basin and along the Amundsen Basin. It comprises a number of seafloor elevations (Lomonosov Ridge and Alpha Ridge) and forms the submerged prolongation of the land mass of Canada. Throughout, the areas of continental shelf extend beyond 200 nautical miles from the territorial sea baselines of Canada and, on the Alpha and Lomonosov Ridges, beyond the 350 nautical mile constraint."

155 The Alpha Ridge extends to the commencement of the Mendeleev Ridge on the other side of the North Pole towards the Russian coast.

156 Randy Boswell, 'Ocean Survey Looks Promising for Arctic Sovereignty Effort', *National Post* (16 May 2008).

157 Pratt (n. 63).

158 1973 Agreement between the Government of the Kingdom of Denmark and the Government of Canada relating to the delimitation of the Continental Shelf between Greenland and Canada, 950 *UNTS* 151.

agreed boundary runs for nearly 1,500 miles from the Davis Strait south to Robeson Channel, at the northern end of Canada's Ellesmere Island and the north east coast of Greenland.[159] The boundary was generally based on equidistance, with a provision for adjustment when new information on the low-water line of Canada's Arctic islands and the Greenland coast became available. The boundary did not, however, fully extend to the north into the Lincoln Sea, north of Ellesmere Island and Greenland. There was an unresolved boundary in respect of continental shelves of approximately 100 nautical miles, and the continental shelf boundary beyond 200 nautical miles from the respective coasts. The 1973 Agreement also did not delimit the boundary for a very small gap of less than one nautical mile in the Nares Strait, relating to the dispute over the sovereignty of Hans Island.

The 1973 Agreement provided for potential adjustments if the agreed boundary was determined not to be based on equidistance, and that neither state would issue petroleum licences in the boundary region without the agreement of the other state on the precise boundary.[160] Canada and Denmark agreed not to delimit the boundary to the north until more was known about the area and its resources.[161] The related issues included whether the Danish Beaumont Island should be given full effect in determining the boundary.[162]

Canada and Denmark announced their tentative agreement to finalise the boundary in the Lincoln Sea to 200 nautical miles from the respective coasts in 2012.[163] This would extend the agreed boundary to approximately 1,600 nautical miles. Both states had negotiated a boundary on the equidistance principle, however, a Danish baseline relating to Beaumont Island had resulted in a dispute over two small areas of approximately 65 nautical square miles in total.[164] The announcement in 2012 did not include agreement on the continental shelf

---

159 Oude Elferink (n. 113) at p. 181.

160 Lewis M Alexander, 'Canada-Denmark (Greenland) Report, Number 1–1', in Charney and Alexander (n. 115) at p. 371.

161 Ibid., at p. 374.

162 Ibid., at p. 376.

163 Government of Canada, Foreign Affairs and International Trade Canada, 'Canada and Kingdom of Denmark Reach Tentative Agreement on Lincoln Sea Boundary', Press Release (28 November 2012) at: http://www.international.gc.ca/media/aff/news-communiques/2012/11/28a.aspx?view=d (last accessed 4 April 2018).

164 Michael Byers has commented that Canada's objection was based on the *Anglo-Norwegian Fisheries Case*, as the baselines were not related to a fringe of islands, were overly long, did not follow the general direction of the coast, and did not cross the intervening fjords but are further offshore. Michael Byers, *Who Owns the Arctic – Understanding Sovereignty in the Far North* (Douglas & McIntyre, Vancouver: 2009) 106.

in the Lincoln Sea. This issue may be resolved in the respective submissions to the CLCS.[165]

Hans Island is a small feature in Nares Strait between Canada's Ellesmere Island and the Danish (Greenland) coast, and is the only disputed land territory in the Arctic Ocean region.[166] The dispute appears to be small in scope; however, there is an issue concerning navigation in the channel between the two coasts. The dispute has a comparatively high profile owing to several incidents, including over-flights and flag plantings.[167] In September 2005 both states issued a joint statement acknowledging their differences, and their commitment to peaceful resolution of the dispute.[168] Hans Island is also significant as proposals to resolve the dispute include each country having sovereignty over half the island, or alternatively making the island a condominium, with shared sovereignty between Canada and Denmark.[169] The condominium proposal potentially relates to a joint development solution relating to land territory of the island.[170] The most significant issue is how the Danish and Greenland Governments' continental shelf submission, and the expected final Canadian submission, may conflict with the revised Russian submission. The Russian submission currently does not extend beyond the North Pole. The potential overlap includes claims which may extend beyond the North Pole on the basis of equidistance, as indicated in the IBRU Arctic map.[171]

3.2.6 Danish Arctic Coast (Greenland) – Lomonosov Ridge

Denmark's sovereignty over Greenland is now uncontested by other states. Danish sovereignty over Eirik Raudes Land in eastern Greenland was unsuccessfully challenged by Norway in the *Legal Status of Eastern Greenland*

---

165 Jacques Hartmann, 'Canada and Denmark reach agreement on the Lincoln Sea Boundary', *EJIL: Talk!* (Blog of the *European Journal of International Law*) (10 January 2013) at: http://www.ejiltalk.org/canada-and-denmark-reach-agreement-on-the-lincoln-sea-boundary/ (last accessed 4 April 2018).

166 Byers (n. 148) at p. 22.

167 Ibid., at p. 26. The incidents included very low over-flight in 1983 by Danish aircraft of a scientific camp established by the Canadian company Dome Petroleum under permit from the Canadian government, Danish flag plantings on the island from 1984 to 2004, a further Canadian survey in 2000, and Canadian flag planting in 2005.

168 Ibid., at p. 28.

169 Ibid. Byers comments that this solution would be similar to the practice adopted for Pheasant Island in the Bidasoa River between France and Spain.

170 Ibid., at p. 30.

171 International Boundaries Research Unit (University of Durham), 'Maritime Jurisdiction and Boundaries in the Arctic Region' (2008) at: http://www.durham.ac.uk/ibru (last accessed 1 March 2018).

(*'Eastern Greenland* case') in 1933.[172] The Permanent Court of International Justice rejected the Norwegian assertion that the territory was *terra nullius*, and confirmed Danish sovereignty, based on assertions of sovereignty and related administrative acts by Denmark. There is currently a significant development towards full independence for Greenland. Home rule government was granted by Denmark in 1979,[173] and this was extended to self-government in 2009.[174]

The Government of Denmark and the Government of Greenland made a partial submission to the CLCS in respect of the northern continental shelf of Greenland on 15 December 2014.[175] The submission is illustrated in Figure 8, and included the area based on the Lomonosov Ridge under the continental shelf provisions of UNCLOS. The submission can be compared to the current claim by Russia, which proceeds from the northern coast of Russia to beyond the North Pole.[176] The Danish and Greenland submission also extends beyond the North Pole, and so substantially overlaps the Russian claim, and also extends into the Arctic Ocean north of the Canadian coast. The Danish and Greenland submission identifies the delimitation issues, including the issue of a future maritime boundary relating to Russia, and provides that the related CLCS recommendations should be without prejudice to the delimitation of the continental shelf.[177] On a similar basis to the Russian continental shelf submission, and the anticipated final Canadian submission, the issue may be determined by whether there is sufficient scientific evidence that the Alpha and Lomonosov Ridges are natural prolongations of the Greenland continental margin.

Denmark made a continental shelf submission in respect of the Faroe Islands in cooperation with the Government of the Faroes in 2009,[178] and

172 *Legal Status of Eastern Greenland* (Denmark v Norway) [1933] PCIJ Rep (Ser. A/B) No. 53.

173 *Home Rule Act of 1979* (Act No 577 of 29 November 1978). These measures included establishment of the Greenland Parliament, *Inatsisartut*.

174 *Greenland Self-Government Act* (Act No 473 of 12 June 2009) at: http://eu.nanoq.gl/Emner/About%20Greenland/Politics%20in%20Greenland.aspx (last accessed 1 March 2018).

175 Commission on the Limits of the Continental Shelf, 'Partial Submission of the Government of the Kingdom of Denmark together with the Government of Greenland to the Commission on the Limits of the Continental Shelf – The Northern Continental Shelf of Greenland' – Executive Summary (2 November 2015) at: http://www.un.org/depts/los/clcs_new/submissions_files/submission_dnk_76_2014.htm (last accessed 4 April 2018).

176 United Nations Commission on the Limits of the Continental Shelf (CLCS) – Revised Russian Submission (1 December 2015) at: http://www.un.org/depts/los/clcs_new/submissions_files/submission_rus_rev1.htm (last accessed 3 April 2018).

177 Ibid., at p. 18.

178 Partial Submission of the Government of the Kingdom of Denmark together with the Government of the Faroes to the Commission on the Limits of the Continental Shelf – The Continental Shelf North of the Faroe Islands (29 April 2009) at: http://www.un.org/

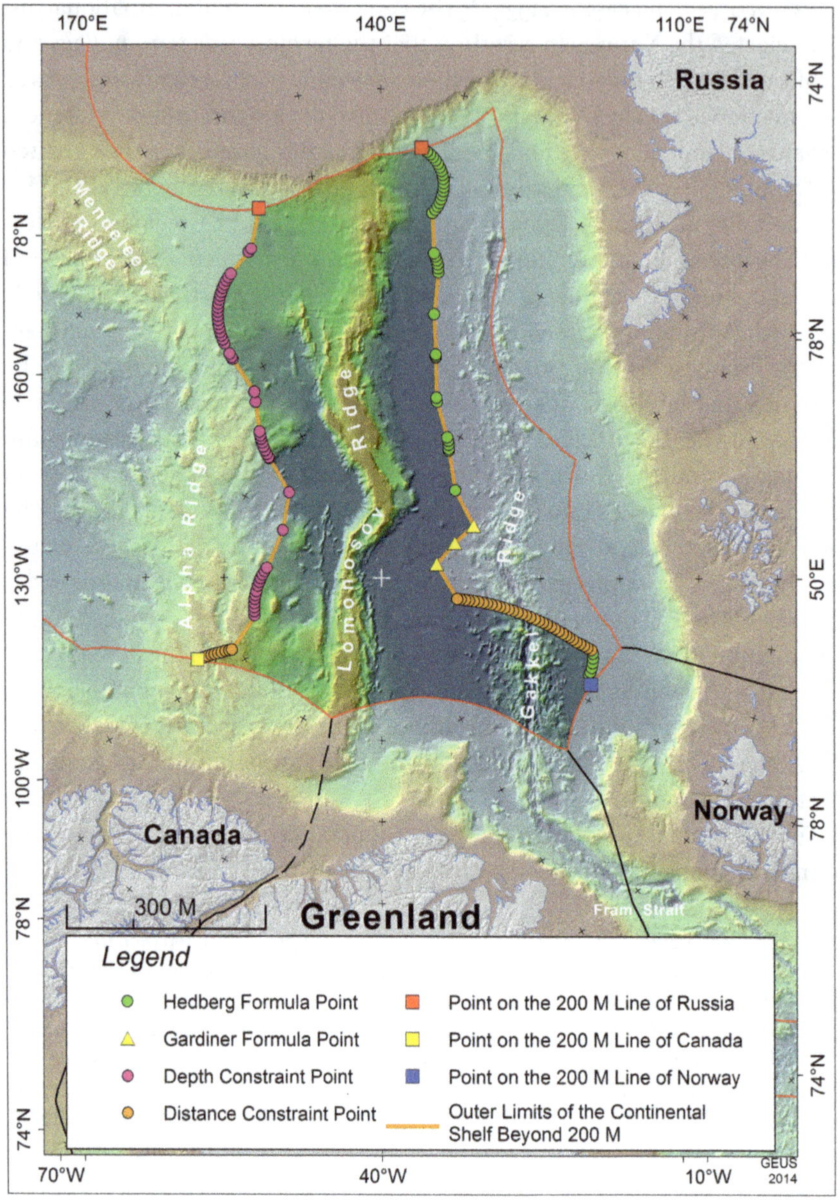

FIGURE 8 Denmark and Greenland continental shelf claim
SOURCE: © GEOLOGICAL SURVEY OF DENMARK AND GREENLAND (GEUS)

a submission together with the Government of Greenland in respect of the southern continental shelf of Greenland in 2012.[179] The Danish boundary of the area south of Greenland is still to be agreed with Canada. The area north-east of Greenland to the Norwegian islands of Jan Mayen and Svalbard, and to the north of Greenland, is still to be agreed with Canada and Russia.[180]

3.2.7 Denmark (Greenland)/Norway (Jan Mayen and Svalbard)

The more southerly Denmark (Greenland) boundary with Norway relating to the Jan Mayen Island region was determined under an Agreement made in 1995,[181] which implemented the ICJ decision in the *Jan Mayen* case.[182] The Norwegian claim was based on a median line, and the Danish claim was based on a 200-nautical-mile boundary, with no effect on Jan Mayen.[183] The ICJ held that a combined boundary should be made generally between these two claims, as an 'equitable solution in the light of relevant circumstances', including lengths of respective coasts and location of fishery resources.[184] Denmark had argued that the boundary should be determined taking into account that Jan Mayen lacked a settled population and an economy, apart from the activities of scientific personnel. The ICJ held that the limited nature of Jan Mayen's population and other socio-economic factors were not circumstances to be taken into account in the delimitation.[185] The 1995 Agreement followed

---

Depts/los/clcs_new/submissions_files/dnk28_09/dnk2009executivesummary.pdf (last accessed 4 April 2018).

179 Partial Submission of the Government of the Kingdom of Denmark together with the Government of Greenland to the Commission on the Limits of the Continental Shelf regarding the Southern Continental Shelf of Greenland, 14 June 2012, at: http://www.un.org/Depts/los/clcs_new/submissions_files/submission_dnk_61_2012.htm (last accessed 4 April 2018).

180 Christian Marcussen et al, 'Exploring for extended continental shelf claims off Greenland and the Faroe Islands – geological perspectives' (2004) 4 *Geological Survey of Denmark and Greenland Bulletin* 61.

181 1995 Agreement between the Government of the Kingdom of Denmark and the Kingdom of Norway relating to the Delimitation of the Continental Shelf in the Area between Jan Mayen and Greenland and of the Boundary between the Fisheries Zones in the Area, 1996 *UNTS* 177.

182 *Case Concerning Maritime Delimitation in the Area between Greenland and Jan Mayen* (Denmark v Norway) Judgement [1993] ICJ Rep 38 (*Jan Mayen Case*).

183 Donald R Rothwell, *The Polar Regions and the Development of International Law* (Cambridge University Press, Cambridge: 1996) 191.

184 The boundary was broadly midway between the 200-nautical-mile boundary for Greenland and the equidistance line. In detail, the southern region 'zone 1' was divided equally, the middle region 'zone 2' and northern region 'zone 3' allowed a somewhat greater allocation to Norway.

185 *Jan Mayen Case* (n. 186).

the ICJ judgment, with minor changes made after consultation with hydrographic experts for a more precise determination of the related baselines. The judgment was the first time that the ICJ drew an equidistance line as the provisional boundary, and then analysed whether that line was equitable.[186]

The more northerly Denmark (Greenland) boundary with Norway relating to the Svalbard Islands region[187] was determined under an Agreement made in 2006.[188] The boundary was based on an equidistance line with a minor adjustment for Denmark's Tobias Island. Denmark has also implicitly recognised Norway's claim that Svalbard generates EEZ and continental shelf zones.[189]

3.2.8 Denmark (Greenland and Faroes)/Iceland

The boundary of the continental shelf between Denmark (Greenland) and Iceland was determined by an Agreement establishing the boundaries of the continental shelf and fisheries zones in 1997.[190] The background to the Agreement included the fisheries dispute relating to the 3,358-square-mile 'grey zone' of overlapping Danish and Icelandic claims relating to the effect to be given to the inhabited Icelandic island of Grimsey and the uninhabited Icelandic islet of Kolbeinsey, and the Danish, Norwegian and Icelandic dispute relating to the 565-square-mile 'Jan Mayen triangle' of respective overlapping claims.

The boundary adopted in the Agreement was generally based on the equidistance line between the respective coasts, giving full effect to Grimsey Island. However, the boundary was adjusted to give limited effect to the Kolbeinsey islet. The agreement resulted in a 70 per cent allocation to Iceland, and 30 per cent allocation to Denmark for the area affected by Kolbeinsey. The states did not define Kolbeinsey to be an island or rock under UNCLOS Article 121.[191]

---

186 DH Anderson, 'Denmark (Greenland) – Norway (Jan Mayen), Report Number 9–19', in Jonathan I Charney, and Lewis M Alexander (eds), *International Maritime Boundaries* Vol 3 (Martinus Nijhoff, Dordrecht/Boston: 1998) 2507.

187 The boundary is north of the Area regime applying in the 'Denmark/Iceland/Norway Banana Hole' discussed below.

188 2006 Agreement between the Government of the Kingdom of Norway on the one hand, and the Government of the Kingdom of Denmark together with the Home Rule Government of Greenland on the other hand, concerning the delimitation of the continental shelf and the fisheries zones in the area between Greenland and Svalbard, 2378 *UNTS* 21.

189 Byers (n. 148) at p. 38.

190 1997 Agreement between the Government of the Kingdom of Denmark, together with the Greenland Home Rule Government, on the one Hand, and the Government of the Republic of Iceland, on the other hand, concerning the Delimitation of the Continental Shelf and the Fishery Zones in the area between Greenland and Iceland, 2074 *UNTS* 58.

191 The result was, however, a small area where potentially no state has EEZ jurisdiction if Kolbeinsey is not treated as an island. The boundary is significant as an example of a compromise between the two states between the island and rock treatments under UNCLOS.

The completion of the Agreement in 1997 enabled Iceland, Denmark (Greenland) and Norway (Jan Mayen) to agree upon a tri-point where the respective maritime boundaries of the three states would meet.[192] This was confirmed by the protocols made in 1997 between Denmark/Norway,[193] and Norway/Iceland.[194] These agreements therefore resolved the 'Jan Mayen triangle' dispute. Anderson has commented that this resolution allocated 35 per cent of the disputed area to Denmark, 35 per cent to Iceland, and 30 per cent to Norway.[195]

An agreement was made in 2006 between Denmark (relating to the Faroes), Iceland and Norway relating to the southern part of the 'Banana Hole' in the North Atlantic.[196] This region is approximately equidistant between the Faroes, Iceland, and Norway, and concerns the region in the southern part of the 'Banana Hole', which is a region beyond coastal state jurisdiction. The agreement included a process for establishing the delimitation of the continental shelf between the States in the area, subject to fulfilment of their internal requirements. On this basis, these states will enter into treaties to extend their boundaries up to the 'Banana Hole' on finalisation of their respective continental shelf submissions. The Denmark (Greenland)/Iceland maritime boundary was extended to the continental shelf by an agreement of January 2013.[197]

---

192 Alex G Oude Elferink, 'Current Legal Developments, Denmark/Iceland/Norway' (1998) 13(4) *International Journal of Marine and Coastal Law* 607.

193 1997 Additional Protocol to the Agreement of 18 December 1995 between the Kingdom of Norway and the Kingdom of Denmark on the Delimitation of the Continental Shelf in the Area between Jan Mayen and Greenland and the Boundary between Fishery Zones in the Area, 2100 *UNTS* 180.

194 1997 Additional Protocol to the Agreement of 28 May 1980 between Norway and Iceland on Fishery and Continental Shelf Questions and the Supplementary Agreement of 22 October 1981 on the Continental Shelf in the Area Between Jan Mayen and Iceland, 2127 *UNTS* 227.

195 DH Anderson, 'Denmark (Greenland) – Iceland', Report Number 9–22', in Jonathan I Charney and Robert W Smith (eds), *International Maritime Boundaries* Vol 4 (Martinus Nijhoff, Dordrecht/London: 2002) 2941, 2944.

196 2006 Agreed Minutes on the Delimitation of the Continental Shelf beyond 200 Nautical Miles between the Faroe Islands, Iceland and Norway in the Southern Part of the Banana Hole of the Northeast Atlantic (20 September 2006) at: https://www.regjeringen.no/en/dokumenter/Agreed-Minutes/id446839/ (last accessed 1 March 2018).

197 2013 Agreed Minutes on the Delimitation of the Continental Shelf beyond 200 Nautical Miles between Greenland and Iceland in the Irminger Sea (16 January 2013) at: http://www.utanrikisraduneyti.is/media/thjodrettarmal/Agreed-Minutes-og-vidaukar.pdf (last accessed 4 April 2018).

3.2.9 Norway (Jan Mayen)/Iceland – Current Arctic JDZ

Iceland and Norway agreed the boundaries in respect of the area within 200 nautical miles of their respective coasts in related agreements in 1980 and 1981.[198] The agreements generally provide a 200-nautical-mile boundary to Iceland, rather than being based on equidistance, and a joint zone straddling the boundary requiring a sharing of resources which lie predominantly on the Norwegian (Jan Mayen) side. The agreements may therefore be considered concessional by Norway.[199]

Norway and Iceland made the Agreement concerning Fishery and Continental Shelf Questions in 1980 (the 1980 Agreement').[200] The 1980 Agreement provided a full 200 nautical miles to Iceland for fisheries purposes, and obtained Iceland's agreement that Norway would have a fishing zone around Jan Mayen outside that area.[201] The 1980 Agreement required the establishment of a Conciliation Commission to recommend the continental shelf boundary. Norway and Iceland entered into the Agreement on the Continental Shelf between Iceland and Jan Mayen in 1981 ('Continental Shelf Agreement') implementing those recommendations.[202]

The Commission recommended the continental shelf boundary be the same as the EEZ and Norway's fishery boundary established by the 1980 Agreement. There should however be a joint zone providing for the sharing of hydrocarbon resources. The joint zone was closer to Jan Mayen than to Iceland, and the majority of the zone is therefore on the Norwegian side of the

198 1980 Agreement between Norway and Iceland on Fishery and Continental Shelf Questions, 2124 *UNTS* 226; 1981 Agreement between Iceland and Norway on the Continental Shelf between Iceland and Jan Mayen, 2124 *UNTS* 262.

199 Alex G Oude Elferink 'Arctic Maritime Delimitations' in Oude Elferink and Rothwell (n. 81), at pp. 179, 183.

200 DH Anderson, 'Iceland-Norway (Jan Mayen), Report Number 9–4', in Jonathan I Charney and Lewis M Alexander (eds), *International Maritime Boundaries* Vol 2 (Martinus Nijhoff, Dordrecht/Boston: 1993) 1755, and Agreement between Norway and Iceland on Fishery and Continental Shelf Questions, 2124 *UNTS* 226.

201 Iceland had considered that Jan Mayen should not affect Iceland's EEZ or continental shelf declared in 1979. Norway had declared a fisheries zone extending from Jan Mayen in 1980, providing however that the boundaries of the zone were to be established by agreement.

202 1981 Agreement between Iceland and Norway on the Continental Shelf between Iceland and Jan Mayen, 2124 *UNTS* 262.

maritime boundary.[203] The Continental Shelf Agreement implemented these recommendations.[204]

Jan Mayen is significant as it was *terra nullius* until claimed by Norway in 1929. The related agreements have confirmed Norway's continental shelf rights arising from Norway's sovereignty over Jan Mayen, and generally reducing the area of Jan Mayen's continental shelf on terms which may be considered as favourable to Iceland. The limited nature of the occupation by Norway, relating primarily to scientific and military missions, supports the position that settlement is not required for the acquisition of territorial sovereignty, consistent with the *Eastern Greenland* case.[205]

The boundary is significant in relation to the Arctic Ocean region as an example of a resource-sharing JDZ. The joint zone extends roughly one-third on the Icelandic side of the boundary, and two-thirds on the Norwegian (Jan Mayen Island) side of the boundary, and broadly provides for the exchange of 25 per cent of the benefits from each state's part of the zone.[206] The joint zone is significant as a case where the maritime boundary was agreed, and so resource sharing was made without potentially undermining the jurisdiction of either state.[207]

3.2.10 Norwegian Arctic Coast and Svalbard Treaty Area

The Svalbard Treaty area is illustrated in Figure 9. The Svalbard Islands are an archipelago located on the Norwegian continental shelf. The Svalbard Islands are subject to the terms of the Svalbard Treaty, which entered into force in 1925.[208] The Treaty established a form of resource sharing including territorial sea resources. However, there is no agreement between Norway and other state parties to the Treaty as to whether the Svalbard Treaty applies to the EEZ or the continental shelf around the islands.[209]

---

203 Anderson (n. 204) at p. 1756. Anderson observed that the Conciliation Commission in its determination commented that 'Iceland is totally dependent on imports of hydrocarbon products'.

204 1981 Agreement between Iceland and Norway on the Continental Shelf between Iceland and Jan Mayen, 2124 *UNTS* 262.

205 *Legal Status of Eastern Greenland* (Denmark v Norway) [1933] PCIJ Rep (Ser. A/B) No. 533.

206 Miyoshi and Schofield (n. 4) at p. 34.

207 There are benefits from this arrangement, particularly enforcement of measures against third states; for example: each state can enforce its own laws for the protection and preservation of the marine environment within its own EEZ and continental shelf.

208 1920 Treaty Concerning the Archipelago Spitsbergen, 2 *LNTS* 8 (Svalbard Treaty).

209 For detailed discussion see generally: Robin Churchill and Geir Ulfstein, *Marine Management in Disputed Areas; The Case of the Barents Sea* (Routledge, London/New York: 1992) 23–53.

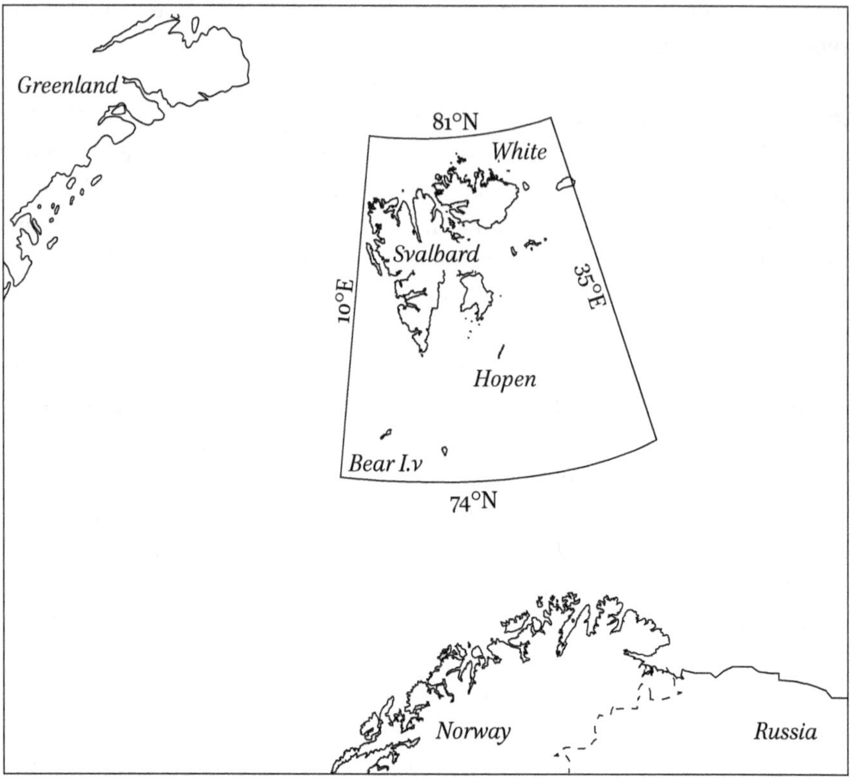

FIGURE 9 Svalbard treaty area
SOURCE: SVALBARD TREATY, AND ROBIN CHURCHILL AND GEIR ULFSTEIN, *MARINE MANAGEMENT IN DISPUTED AREAS* (1992)

Norwegian sovereignty over the Svalbard Islands is based on the Svalbard Treaty.[210] The islands had been the location of Dutch, English Danish and French settlements to support whaling from 1611 as well as Norwegian and Russian hunting activities, and Norwegian, British and American coal interests from 1899.[211] Svalbard is of particular interest in respect of JDZs as competing claims were resolved by a multilateral regime allowing access to land and territorial sea resources. That access is provided under the state sovereignty of Norway, which provides effective management of the islands,

210 See generally: Geir Ulfstein, *The Svalbard Treaty: From* Terra Nullius *to Norwegian Sovereignty* (Scandinavian University Press, Oslo: 1995).

211 The Governor of Svalbard, 'Historical background', at: http://www.sysselmannen.no/en/Toppmeny/About-Svalbard/Historical-background/ (last accessed 4 April 2018).

including the enforcement of measures for the protection and preservation of the environment.

Norway has defined the limits of the continental shelf in the *Act Pertaining to Petroleum Activities* of 1985.[212] The limits are defined as the seabed and subsoil outside Norwegian territorial sea, as far as it can be regarded as a natural prolongation of the Norwegian land territory but no less than 200 nautical miles from the baseline from which the territorial sea is measured, but not beyond the median line in relation to other states. The issue of state rights to oil and gas on the continental shelf of Svalbard is primarily a question of treaty interpretation: specifically, whether the Svalbard Treaty should apply to the EEZ and continental shelf regimes not existing at the time of the treaty's adoption.

The Vienna Convention on the Law of Treaties (VCLT)[213] may give rise to a static or dynamic approach to treaty interpretation. The principal clause relevant to Svalbard is Article 31, which requires that a treaty be interpreted 'in good faith in accordance with the ordinary meaning to be given to the terms of the treaty in their context and in the light of its objects and purpose.' The issue in relation to Svalbard is whether the Svalbard Treaty should be interpreted to include the juridical continental shelf in the terms 'waters' and 'territorial waters' used in the Treaty,[214] notwithstanding the fact that the continental shelf regime did not exist at the time of the adoption of the Svalbard Treaty. Norway has not, however, acceded to the VCLT[215] and the VCLT does not in any case have retrospective effect.

Caracciolo has commented on the principle of effectiveness in treaty interpretation: 'Under this principle the norms set by a treaty must be interpreted in a manner that gives them meaning and effect, or at least partial effect.'[216] This principle of treaty interpretation is argued to override the restrictive interpretation adopted by Norway, because the purpose of the Treaty was to grant Norway sovereignty, subject to limiting sovereignty with respect to maintaining the freedoms of other states. It may be considered that to give effectiveness

212 *Act of 22 March 1985 No 11 Pertaining to Petroleum Activities* (Norway) at: http://www.un.org/Depts/los/legislationandtreaties/statefiles/Nor.html (last accessed 1 March 2018).

213 1969 Vienna Convention on the Law of Treaties, 1155 *UNTS* 331 (VCLT).

214 Article 3, VCLT.

215 Torbjørn Pedersen, 'The Svalbard Continental Shelf Controversy: Legal Disputes and Political Rivalries' (2006) 37(3) *Ocean Development and International Law* 339, 345.

216 Ida Caracciolo, 'Unresolved controversy: the legal situation of the Svalbard Islands maritime areas; an interpretation of the Paris Treaty in light of UNCLOS 1982' (Paper presented at The State of Sovereignty International Boundary Research Unit Conference, Durham, 2 April 2009) at: http://www.dur.ac.uk/resources/ibru/conferences/sos/ida_caracciolo_paper.pdf (last accessed 4 April 2018).

to this purpose, the Treaty should therefore also apply to resources of the EEZ and the continental shelf.

There is also an issue of intertemporal law, which concerns which law should apply given that facts and laws change over time.[217] The issue most commonly concerns the interpretation of treaties, and particularly whether the interpretation of treaties should adopt a static or an evolutionary approach. The static approach requires application to the facts and laws at the time the treaty was made. The evolutionary approach can allow application of the terms of a treaty taking into account the facts and circumstances after the effective date of the treaty. This may apply, for example, by attributing the current meaning of words, rather than the meaning at the time the treaty was made.[218] The ICJ adopted the intertemporal principle in the case on the *Continental Shelf in the Aegean Sea* case in 1978.[219]

Anderson observed that 'the task is to identify rights and obligations of Norway and those of other parties by interpreting the words used in their context and in the light of the object and purpose of the treaty.'[220] The expressed intention of the Svalbard Treaty was to provide Svalbard with an 'equitable regime' in order to ensure its development and utilisation. This intention was realised by conferring sovereignty on Norway, subject to the fishing and mining rights to be enjoyed by all parties. On this basis other states should have economic rights to the Svalbard continental shelf.[221] This is consistent with the view of Robin Churchill and Geir Ulfstein, who state in summary that Norway has full sovereignty over Svalbard and all maritime areas around Svalbard,

217 Boleslaw A Boczek, *International Law: A Dictionary* (Scarecrow Press, Lanham: 2005) 227, defines intertemporal law as follows:

"The term intertemporal law refers to the principles of international law dealing with the problem of which of the different rules of international law prevailing in succeeding periods are to govern a specific situation."

218 Andrew Clapham, *Brierly's Law of Nations, An Introduction to the Role of International Law in International Relations* 7th ed (Oxford University Press, Oxford: 2012) 357.

219 *Continental Shelf in the Aegean Sea* (Greece v Turkey) [1978] ICJ Rep p. 3. In that case, exclusion of the application of the Geneva General Act for the Settlement of Disputes to disputes on the 'territorial status of Greece', was held by the ICJ to include a reservation on disputes on the continental shelf.

220 DH Anderson, 'The Status under International Law of the Maritime Areas around Svalbard' (2009) 40(4) *Ocean Development and International Law* 373, at p. 380.

221 Ibid., at p. 381. Anderson commented:

"To interpret the reference to Norway's sovereignty in an ambulatory way so as to apply not only to the land and the original territorial waters, but also to the extended territorial sea, continental shelf, fisheries zone and, at the same time, to interpret the reference to other states' rights strictly so that the rights were confined to the land and the original territorial sea would hardly be equitable or balanced."

but the Svalbard Treaty applies to all such areas.[222] There is, accordingly, support to conclude that there are substantial grounds for rights of other states to resources of the Svalbard continental shelf, including offshore oil and gas.

The Denmark (Greenland)/Norway agreement, adopted in 2006, in part relates to the Svalbard region.[223] As discussed above, Byers considered that Denmark implicitly recognised Norway's claim that Svalbard generates EEZ and continental shelf zones by entering into the agreement.[224] The agreement does not, however, contain any provision relating to potential resource sharing and the Svalbard Treaty. There has been some acceptance by other states that Norway can negotiate maritime zones around Svalbard.[225] Molenaar considered that the acceptance by other states that Norway can negotiate maritime zones around Svalbard did not extend to excluding other states' access to the continental shelf surrounding Svalbard.[226]

The European Union has not accepted Norwegian claims to an EEZ relating to Svalbard. The European Union has, however, protested over the Norwegian exercise of fishery laws in the EEZ around Svalbard, including Norwegian measures against the Spanish fishing vessels *Olazar* and *Olaberri* in 2004, and the Portuguese vessel *Praia de Santa Cruz* in 2009.[227] Iceland and Russia have been described as the 'most vigorous opponents of Norway's view' by Pedersen. This opposition is made on the basis that Norwegian sovereignty over Svalbard is founded on a treaty rather than customary law. Norwegian sovereignty granted by the 1920 Treaty, in this view, 'is curtailed both geographically and in scope, and consequently does not provide to Norway a coastal state's legal access to claim or enforce a 200 nautical mile fisheries protection zone in the waters around Svalbard, or to claim jurisdiction on the continental shelf adjacent to Svalbard.'[228]

In relation to the commercial development of the region, Norway announced an oil and gas exploration licence program south of Svalbard in the Barents

222 Churchill and Ulfstein (n. 213) at p. 53.

223 2006 Agreement between the Government of the Kingdom of Norway on the one hand, and the Government of the Kingdom of Denmark together with the Home Rule Government of Greenland on the other hand, concerning the delimitation of the continental shelf and the fisheries zones in the area between Greenland and Svalbard, 2378 *UNTS* 21.

224 Byers (n. 148) at p. 38.

225 EJ Molenaar, 'Fisheries Regulation in the Maritime Zones of Svalbard' (2012) 27 *International Journal of Marine and Coastal Law* 3, at p. 20.

226 Ibid. This included Russia issuing a *Note Verbale* in response to Norway's submission to the CLCS, which provided that the recommendations of the CLCS in response to Norway's submission should be without prejudice to the Spitzbergen Treaty.

227 Ibid., at p. 23.

228 Pedersen (n. 219) at p. 345.

Sea South program in 1989, which partially extended into the Svalbard Treaty area.[229] No exploration licences had, however, been granted in the Svalbard area north of 74° north.[230] Denmark has resolved maritime boundaries between Greenland and Norway surrounding Svalbard, but maintains that Norway does not have sole sovereign rights to the resources of the related maritime zones due to the Svalbard Treaty.[231]

The scope of the Svalbard Treaty is therefore not yet determined, and there are strong arguments that the regime of multilateral access to resources under the Treaty should also apply to the continental shelf. The issue of rights to oil and gas resources of the continental shelf of Svalbard is one of the most significant areas of potential conflicting claims to oil and gas resources.

Norway made a partial CLCS submission in respect of the Arctic for areas in the Norwegian and Barents Seas on 27 November 2006, including the Western Nansen Basin region north of Svalbard.[232] The CLCS recommendation made on 27 March 2009 was stated to be 'without prejudice to matters relating to delimitation between States, or application of other parts of the Convention or any other treaties.'[233] Accordingly, the CLCS recommendation did not make any finding in relation to the Svalbard Treaty. A CLCS determination of the limits of the continental shelf would leave the dispute unresolved.[234]

3.2.11 Norway/Russia (Barents Sea) – Resolved by the 2010 Treaty

The dispute between Norway and Russia over the maritime boundary in the Barents Sea was resolved by the boundary treaty signed on 15 September 2010 ('Barents Sea Treaty').[235] The Norwegian claim prior to the 2010 Barents Sea Treaty was based on equidistance, whereas the Russian claim was based on

229 The Barents Sea South program extended to 74°30' N in 1989, with 30' of the licence area extending into the Svalbard Treaty area.

230 Pedersen (n. 219) at p. 347.

231 Torbjørn Pedersen, 'Denmark's Policies toward the Svalbard Area' (2009) 40(4) *Ocean Development and International Law* 319.

232 Continental Shelf Submission of Norway in respect of areas in the Arctic Ocean, the Barents Sea and the Norwegian Sea (27 November 2006) at: https://www.un.org/depts/los/clcs_new/submissions_files/submission_nor.htm (last accessed 4 April 2018).

233 Summary of the Recommendations of the Commission on the Limits of the Continental Shelf In Regard To the Submission Made By Norway in Respect of Areas in the Arctic Ocean, the Barents Sea and the Norwegian Sea On 27 November 2006, 2, at: http://www.un.org/Depts/los/clcs_new/submissions_files/nor06/nor_rec_summ.pdf (last accessed 4 April 2018).

234 Pedersen (n. 219) at p. 352.

235 2010 Treaty Between the Kingdom of Norway and the Russian Federation Concerning Maritime Delimitation and Cooperation in the Barents Sea and the Arctic Ocean, 2791 *UNTS* I-49095.

a boundary running to the north of the land boundary on the basis of the sector principle. The result was a disputed area of 175,000 square kilometres. There had been negotiations towards a boundary compromise, including the possible use of a JDZ.[236] The proposal was rejected by Norway in line with its policy of opposing common management schemes with the Soviet Union.[237] The Russian claim for the sector principle was based on special circumstances, including population size, economic interests, and the Svalbard Treaty, as a result of which it was claimed the islands should not be given the status which would otherwise be accorded to Norwegian territory. There were no precedents for factors such as population size or economic interest as special circumstances to support not using equidistance as the basis for the boundary.[238]

Tore Henriksen and Geir Ulfstein observed that neither the joint statement issued by the Norwegian and Russian governments nor the Barents Sea Treaty describe the basis of delimitation adopted in the Treaty.[239] There was no indication of whether geographical circumstances such as the coastline or the undersea prolongation of the continental shelf determined the boundary.[240] The Joint Statement issued by Norway and Russia referred to the Treaty as dividing the disputed area into 'two parts of approximately the same size'.[241] The Russian Foreign Ministry stated that the agreement gave approximately 88,000 square kilometres to each state.[242] This may suggest that achieving an approximately equal division of the disputed area was the primary objective of the Barents Sea Treaty. Norway described the result as a modified median line, and Russia described the result as a modified sector line.[243] A Joint Operating Agreement is required for the exploitation of the trans-boundary hydrocarbon deposits.[244]

---

236 Oude Elferink (n. 113) at p. 185.

237 Alex G Oude Elferink, *The law of maritime boundary delimitation: a case study of the Russian Federation* (Martinus Nijhoff, Dordrecht/Boston: 1994) 240.

238 Ibid., at p. 187.

239 Tore Henriksen and Geir Ulfstein, 'Maritime Delimitation in the Arctic: The Barents Sea Treaty' (2011) 42 *Ocean Development and International Law* 1.

240 Howard Amos, 'Arctic Treaty with Norway Opens Fields', *Moscow Times* (7 July 2011) at: http://old.themoscowtimes.com/business/article/arctic-treaty-with-norway-opens-fields/440178.html (last accessed 3 April 2018).

241 'Joint Statement on Maritime Delimitation and Cooperation in the Barents Sea and the Arctic Ocean', in Henriksen and Ulfstein (n. 243) at p. 10.

242 Ibid.

243 This has some significance as giving support to the sector principle, which is relevant to Russia's other Arctic claim, and to the Argentine claim in the Southern Ocean.

244 Article 5 and Annex II, 2010 Treaty between the Kingdom of Norway and the Russian Federation Concerning Maritime Delimitation and Cooperation in the Barents Sea and the Arctic Ocean.

The Barents Sea Treaty also provides for the transfer of EEZ rights from Norway to Russia in a small 'special area' east of the boundary, but within 200 nautical miles of the Vardø region of north-eastern Norway, to prevent the related fishery resources being subject to neither state's jurisdiction.[245] This is similar to the arrangements in the 1990 United States/Russia boundary agreement.[246] Oil and gas are already being exploited in the Barents Sea.

3.2.12 Russian Arctic Coast – Lomonosov and Mendeleev Ridges

Russia declared baselines for the Arctic Ocean region in the Decree of 15 January 1985 of the Council of Ministers of the Soviet Union.[247] The Russian baselines were declared around a series of Arctic Ocean islands,[248] and enclosed several straits.[249] The United States position was that the Russian baseline was contrary to international law as it purported to treat international straits as internal waters. United States actions included the voyage of the United States submarine USS *Baton Rouge* to protest the baseline closing access to Murmansk in 1992.[250]

Russia ratified UNCLOS on 12 March 1997, and made a submission to the CLCS in 2001. The submission included a continental shelf extending in parts to the North Pole.[251] The CLCS adopted recommendations on the claim in June 2002, including requesting a revised submission in relation to the Arctic.[252] The CLCS received *note verbale* responses from Canada, Denmark, Japan,

245 Article 3, 2010 Treaty between the Kingdom of Norway and the Russian Federation Concerning Maritime Delimitation and Cooperation in the Barents Sea and the Arctic Ocean. IBRU commented that this arrangement is similar to an area created under the USA and Russia Bering Sea Treaty in 1990: International Boundaries Research Unit (University of Durham), 'Maritime jurisdiction and boundaries in the Arctic Region' (n.d.) Note 5, at: http://www.dur.ac.uk/resources/ibru/arctic (last accessed 4 April 2018).

246 1990 Agreement between the United States of America and the Union of Soviet Socialist Republics on the Maritime Boundary, United States, Department of State, at: http://www.state.gov/documents/organization/125431.pdf (last accessed 4 April 2018) (United States/Russia 1990 Agreement).

247 Decree of 15 January 1985 of the Council of Ministers of the Soviet Union (4450 Declaration).

248 Scovazzi (n. 154) at p. 76.

249 Ibid. The baselines enclosed the Shokalski, Vilkitski, Sannikov and Dmitri Laptev straits as Russian internal waters.

250 Ibid., at p. 83.

251 Ron Macnab, 'Submarine Elevations and Ridges: Wild Cards in the Poker Game of UNCLOS Article 76' (2008) 39(2) *Ocean Development and International Law* 223, at p. 226.

252 Commission on the Limits of the Continental Shelf, 'Statement by the Chairman of the Commission on the Limits of the Continental Shelf on the progress of work in the Commission' (24–28 June 2002) UN Doc. CLCS/34, 33.

Norway and the United States.[253] Canada's response in 2002 was that it was unable to respond without further supporting data, and the response was not agreement with or acquiescence in the Russian submission. The submission and CLCS recommendation would be without prejudice to boundary delimitation between Canada and Russia. The Danish and Greenland Government submissions made in 2014 overlap the Russian claim, and the anticipated final Canadian continental shelf submission may also overlap the Russian claim. Russia provided the revised partial submission in relation to the Arctic Ocean on 3 August 2015. The revised partial submission is also based on the Lomonosov and Mendeleev ridges; however, the revised partial submission extends beyond the North Pole.[254]

The revised Russian continental shelf claim is illustrated in Figure 10. The Russian submission included areas adjacent to the Lomonosov and Mendeleev Ridges. The likely basis of the claim is that the ridges are 'natural prolongations' of the Russian continental shelf, and which therefore gave rise to a claim to resources, such as oil and gas, extending on either side of the ridges.[255] The revised Russian submission extended beyond the North Pole along the Lomonosov ridge.

The Russian claim was highlighted in August 2007 by the planting of the Russian flag on the sea floor at the North Pole, more than two and a half miles below the ocean surface. The flag was placed by two mini-submersibles launched from the research ship *Akademik Fyodorov*.[256] The former Soviet Union had placed its flag on ice at the surface of the North Pole in an expedition by the

253 Commission on the Limits of the Continental Shelf (CLCS) – Outer limits of the continental shelf beyond 200 nautical miles from the baselines: Submissions to the Commission: Submission by the Russian Federation, at: http://www.un.org/Depts/los/clcs_new/submissions_files/submission_rus.htm (last accessed 4 April 2018).

254 Partial Revised Submission of the Russian Federation to the Commission on the Limits of the Continental Shelf in respect of the Continental Shelf of the Russian Federation in the Arctic Ocean (3 August 2015) at: http://www.un.org/depts/los/clcs_new/submissions_files/submission_rus_rev1.htm (last accessed 4 April 2018), and International Boundary Research Unit (University of Durham), 'Russia submits new Arctic Ocean claim' (4 November 2014) at: https://www.dur.ac.uk/ibru/news/boundary_news (last accessed 2 March 2018).

255 Commission on the Limits of the Continental Shelf, Russian Federation submission through the Secretary-General to the Commission on the Limits of the Continental Shelf, pursuant to article 76, paragraph 8, of the Convention (20 December 2001) at: https://www.un.org/depts/los/clcs_new/submissions_files/submission_rus.htm (last accessed 4 April 2018) (Russian Submission).

256 'The Arctic – Gold Rush under the Ice', *The Economist* (3 August 2007).

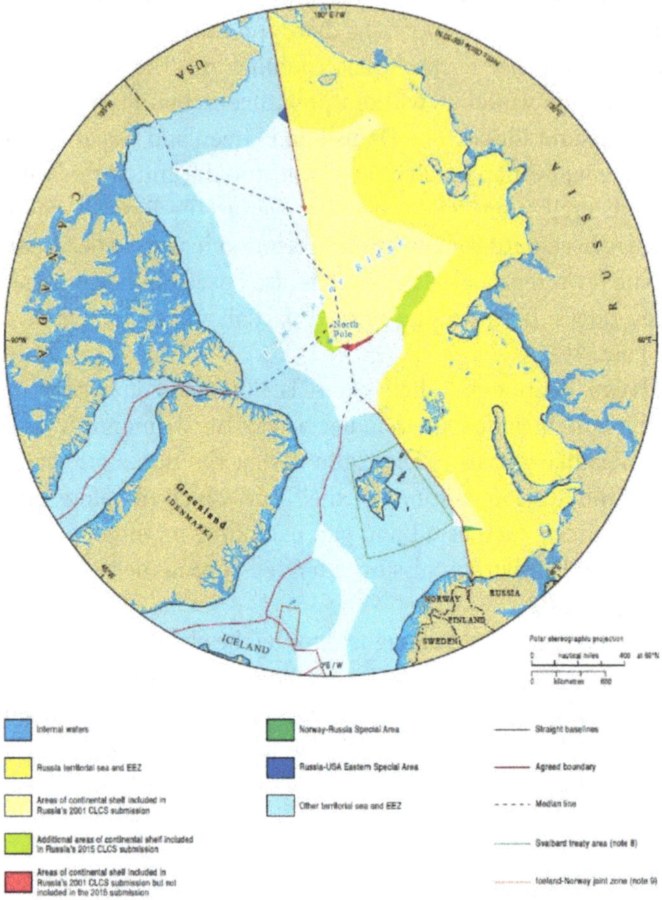

FIGURE 10 Russian revised continental shelf claim
SOURCE: IBRU, DURHAM UNIVERSITY, UK HTTPS://WWW.DUR.AC.UK/IBRU/RESOURCES/ARCTIC/

ice-breaker *Arktica* in 1977.[257] It is generally agreed that the Russian action in 2007 was not legally significant in terms of UNCLOS, as Russia has made a submission to the CLCS to determine the extent of the continental shelf. The Denmark and Greenland Government submissions do, however, extend in the direction of Russia beyond the North Pole. There may be a dispute where

257 RK Headland, 'Ships That Have Reached The North Pole', *Polar Information Sheets* (Scott Polar Research Institute, University of Cambridge) (17 August 2017) at: https://www.spri.cam.ac.uk/resources/infosheets/northpoleships.pdf (last accessed 4 April 2018).

boundaries are not then agreed between the states in this region: for example, where a Canadian claim was based on equidistance as indicated in the IBRU Arctic map.[258]

Following the flag-planting incident, Denmark invited the other Arctic states to a conference in Ilulissat in Greenland. All five Arctic states reaffirmed their commitment to working together within an existing framework of international law in the Ilulissat Declaration in May 2008.[259] One aspect of the flag planting was seen as significant from a Canadian perspective, being a demonstration of Russian capability in the Arctic Ocean.[260] The Russian Government has stated the general basis of the continental shelf claim, without reference to specific UNCLOS provisions.[261] The technical basis for a CLCS submission and related deliberations are confidential. Nevertheless, there are grounds that could potentially support the Russian claim extending several hundred nautical miles north from the Russian Arctic coast.[262]

The United States response to the Russian submission is that regardless of the continental origin, at present the Lomonosov Ridge does not amount to a natural prolongation of either the Russian continental margin or the margins off Greenland or Ellesmere Island.[263] In this interpretation, even if the CLCS concluded that the geological origin of the Lomonosov Ridge related to the

258 Pratt (n. 63).

259 Byers (n. 148) at p. 89.

260 Ken S Coates, P Whitney Lackenbauer, William R Morrison et al., *Arctic Front – Defending Canada in the Far North* (Thomas Allen & Son, Toronto: 2008) 162.

261 Tomasz Górski, 'A Note on Submarine Ridges and Elevations with Special Reference to the Russian Federation and the Arctic Ridges' (2009) 40(1) *Ocean Development and International Law* 51; and Statement Made by the Deputy Minister for Natural Resources of the Russian Federation During Presentation of the Submission Made by the Russian Federation to the Commission on 28 March 2002, Doc. CLCS/31, (5 April 2002) 5. The Russian presentation stated:

"The results of the interpretation of comprehensive geological and geophysical data support the categorization of the Amerasian basin geostructures (Lomonosov ridge and Mendeleev and Alpha rises) as components of the continental margin ... The conclusion regarding the continental nature of the earth's crust was also made on the basis of the interpretation of seismic data (deep seismic sounding and seismic reflection sounding) ... The earth's crust is up to 32 km thick and contains typical components of the continental crust (sedimentary layer up to 5 km thick, upper crust up to 6–8 km thick, with velocity reversal (waveguides) in the lower part, and lower crust up to 20 km thick). This data is independently confirmed by the results of density modelling."

262 Marc Benitah, 'Russia's Claim in the Arctic and the Vexing Issue of Ridges in UNCLOS' (2007) *ASIL Insight* 11; Macnab (n. 255) at p. 226, and Russian Submission (n. 259).

263 Mel Weber, 'Defining the Outer Limits of the Continental Shelf across the Arctic Basin: The Russian Submission, States' Rights, Boundary Delimitation and Arctic Regional Cooperation' (2009) 24 *International Journal of Marine and Coastal Law* 653, at p. 661. Weber

Russian, Canadian or Greenland continents, the Ridge would not be a 'natural prolongation' as required by Article 76(1). In this respect, the United States response referred to morphological breaks from the continental margins.[264]

The terms 'submarine elevations' and 'natural components' are not defined in UNCLOS, with the result that the CLCS may have to determine the meaning of these terms in considering the Russian continental shelf claim. The CLCS may therefore be required to analyse whether the Lomonosov and Mendeleev Ridges are 'oceanic ridges', and, if that is the case, reject that portion of the Russian claim.[265] The International Law Association (ILA) has considered whether state practice or CLCS interpretations have clarified these terms.[266] The ILA did not provide a recommended definition of the term; however, it concluded that all submarine ridges should be limited to 350 nautical miles. The ILA also concluded that the inclusion of paragraph 6 in Article 76 was intended to limit the continental shelf to 350 nautical miles on submarine ridges and this is confirmed by a number of commentaries on the negotiations.[267]

---

commented on the Canada, Denmark, Japan, Norway and the United States responses as follows:

"The Notes Verbales of the five states addressed several different aspects. These include the difficulty of assessing proposed outer limits given the current state of knowledge, problems of overlapping jurisdiction, questionable baselines and differences in the geological interpretation of the central Arctic Ocean."

264 Macnab (n. 255) at p. 226.

265 Benitah (n. 266) at p. 271.

266 International Law Association, Outer Continental Shelf Committee of the International Law Association (ILA), (Berlin Conference 2004) at: http://www.ila-hq.org/en/committees/index.cfm/cid/33 (last accessed 1 March 2018). The chair and co-rapporteurs were Judge Dolliver Nelson, Dr David Ong and Dr Alex G Oude Elferink. The comments relating to Article 76(6) and submarine elevations which can form part of the continental shelf, and are not limited to the 350-mile limit included the following:
- Article 76(6) was not intended to detract from Article 76(3) of the Convention, which excludes 'oceanic ridges' from the continental margin;
- Any interpretation of Articles 76(3) and 76(6) has to take into account the object and purpose of Article 76 as a whole. Article 76(1) indicates that the continental shelf is the natural prolongation of the land territory to the outer edge of the continental margin;
- The drafting history of Article 76(6) lends support to the interpretation that ridges of an oceanic origin may be covered by the provision on submarine ridges; and,
- The view that the inclusion of paragraph 6 in Article 76 was intended to limit the continental shelf to 350 nautical miles on submarine ridges is confirmed by a number of commentaries on the negotiations.

267 Ibid. at p. 21, footnote 101. The ILA referred to T Treves, 'La Nona Sessione della Conferenza sul Diritto del Mare' (1980) 63 *Rivista di Diritto Internazionale* 432–463 at p. 437; E Miles, *Global Ocean Politics* (Martinus Nijhoff, The Hague: 1998) 387–388; ED Brown, *Sea-Bed Energy and Minerals: The International Legal Regime; Vol 1 The Continental Shelf* (Martinus

The region has large potential oil and gas reserves. Significant Arctic oil and gas developments include the Yamal LNG project, which includes the planned commissioning of sixteen icebreaker tankers for transport via the Northern Sea Route to markets including China.[268] These developments also include the Prirazlomnoye oil field in the Pechora Sea, which includes an Arctic-class ice-resistant oil platform.[269] The potential oil and gas reserves include the Kara Sea north of the Russian coast, the Arctic Ocean north of Franz Joseph Land, and the Barents Sea towards the Norwegian coast.[270]

3.2.13 The Area – UNCLOS Part XI Regime

The Area regime is likely to include central areas in the Arctic Ocean (shown as two unshaded areas in the IBRU Arctic Boundary Map),[271] the Bering Sea between the United States and Russia ('Central Bering Sea Doughnut Hole'), the Barents Sea north of Norway and Russia ('Norway/Russia Loop-hole'), and the Norwegian Sea between the Norwegian coast and Jan Mayen ('Denmark/Iceland/Norway Banana Hole').[272] The coordinates of the Area have yet to be determined as the continental shelf has yet to be delimited. The Area regime in the Arctic Ocean, in particular, may be significantly larger than illustrated if the CLCS does not recommend continental shelf areas relating to the Lomonosov and Alpha/Mendeleev Ridges. The principal issue is whether measures such as protection of the environment can be effectively enforced in separate areas surrounded by Arctic states. It is arguable that harmonised measures should be adopted consistent with Arctic Council standards, such as the Arctic Marine Oil Pollution Preparedness and Response regime.[273] The regions subject to the Area regime represent the furthest sea depths from

---

Nijhoff Publishers, Dordrecht: 1992) 31; and SA Meese, 'The Legal Regime Governing Polymetallic Sulfide Deposits' (1986) 17 *Ocean Development and International Law* 131–162 at pp. 145–146.

268 Total S.A., 'Yamal LNG, A Gas Project Like No Other' (n.d.) at: https://www.total.com/en/media/video/yamal-lng-gas-project-no-other (last accessed 2 March 2018).

269 Gazprom, 'Prirazlomnoye oil field'(n.d.) at: http://www.gazprom.com/about/production/projects/deposits/pnm/ (last accessed 4 April 2018). The development was the site of a significant Greenpeace protest in 2013. 'Russians Fire Shots amid Greenpeace Arctic Protest', *Rigzone* (18 September 2013) at:http://www.rigzone.com/news/oil_gas/a/129108/Russians_Fire_Shots_amid_Greenpeace_Arctic_Protest (last accessed 4 April 2018).

270 Green and Kaplan (n. 12) at p. 81.

271 Pratt (n. 63).

272 Oude Elferink and Rothwell (n. 81) at p. 351.

273 Arctic Council, Senior Arctic Officials (SAO) Report to Ministers, Nuuk, Greenland (May 2011) 4.

state continental shelves, and therefore await seismic research and exploratory drilling to determine whether there are economic oil and gas reserves.

3.3 *Areas Suitable for JDZs*

The establishment of JDZs has been successful in several regions and has allowed cooperation between states notwithstanding competing continental shelf claims and allowed the development of offshore oil and gas resources based on the sharing of resources. The Arctic Ocean region has significant potential oil and gas reserves with the opportunity for resource sharing to manage resource conflicts in the region.[274] As discussed above, there are several regions of overlapping claims which may therefore be considered for the potential application of JDZs. These regions generally have geographical or historical circumstances which have resulted in one or more of the states concerned not having adopted an equidistance-based claim. These regions are the maritime boundaries of the United States with Canada and Russia, the potential continental shelf overlap of Denmark (Greenland), Canada and Russia, and the Svalbard Islands. Implementation of JDZs is also subject to the process of the CLCS in reviewing continental shelf submissions.

3.3.1 United States and Russia – Bering Sea

A primary area for a potential JDZ lies in the Bering Sea between the United States and Russia, extending north to the Chukchi Sea and the Arctic Ocean. The United States and Russia signed an Agreement on the Maritime Boundary on 1 June 1990,[275] to delimit the baselines and continental shelf in the Bering and Chukchi Seas into the Arctic Ocean. The United States ratified the Agreement on 16 September 1991. Russia has not ratified the Agreement; however, the two states have agreed to apply the Agreement provisionally.[276] Russia may, however, ratify the Agreement at a later date, in which case no JDZ would be required.[277]

274 The most significant Arctic Ocean and adjoining regions based on potential oil and gas reserves are between the United States and Russia in the Bering Sea, the United States and Canada in the Beaufort Sea, the Central Arctic region between Canada, Denmark (Greenland) and Russia, and the Svalbard Islands region in the Greenland and Barents Seas and Arctic Ocean. The most significant Southern Ocean regions based on potential oil and gas reserves, subject to the very limited drilling to date, are the Weddell Sea region claimed by the United Kingdom, Argentina and Chile, the Ross Sea in the New Zealand Ross Dependency, and Prydz Bay in the Australian Antarctic Territory.

275 1990 Agreement (n. 111).

276 Oude Elferink (n. 113) at p. 183.

277 There is an issue whether the implementation of a future Bering Sea JDZ would be affected when the United States has acceded to UNCLOS. This issue raises concern in

3.3.2 United States and Canada – Beaufort Sea

The Beaufort Sea between the United States and Canada also has potential for a JDZ. The disputed area is not large; however, oil exploration is actively conducted in this region. In this case Canada's claim appears to be quite strong, and the Canadian government may prefer to refer the matter for arbitration under UNCLOS in the event that the United States accedes to UNCLOS. However, a corresponding concession may also be offered by the United States to support a JDZ. One example would be United States recognition of the Northwest Passage as Canadian internal waters rather than an international strait. Joint development solutions have been proposed for this region, including Canadian management of the region under a joint development agreement, with a portion of the related profits paid to the United States.[278]

3.3.3 Svalbard

Svalbard is potentially one of the more complex maritime boundary disputes in the Arctic Ocean region owing to the issue of the applicability of the Svalbard Treaty as discussed above.[279] The principal issues concerning a JDZ relating to Svalbard are that a continental shelf JDZ needs the agreement of the states concerned, and any sharing of resources beyond the territorial sea is currently contrary to Norway's view that it has sole rights to the resources of the Svalbard continental shelf. The determination of a way forward is likely to be a complex matter; however, one method may be to recognise some part of the Norwegian claim, in return for Norway's exercise of effective regulatory authority. It would be a reasonable exercise of Norwegian sovereignty to require any state proposing to engage in JDZ arrangements to accept ultimate oversight and control of these arrangements by Norway.

One possible solution may be an equal sharing between Norway and the contractor states: for example, by allowing Norway the right to tax 50 per cent of the income from operations in the Svalbard continental shelf, and allowing the state of residence of the operators the right to tax 50 per cent of the remaining income. Norway's powers to tax are limited under Article 8 of the Svalbard

---

relation to UNCLOS measures for dispute resolution, and for protection and preservation of the marine environment.

278 Byers (n. 148) at p. 89.

279 Article 3, Svalbard Treaty provides to all parties:

"equal liberty of access and entry for any reason or object whatever to the waters, fjords and ports of the territories ... They hall be admitted under the same conditions of equality to the exercise and practice of all maritime, industrial, mining or commercial enterprises both on land and in the territorial waters ..."

Treaty,[280] and accordingly such taxation provisions of a potential new agreement for a JDZ would need to replace these terms. Norway would be required to licence oil companies providing they met the required standards, particularly the environmental standards. It would remain to be determined whether other states would consider the structure to be acceptable, recognising that Norwegian arguments for resources have some basis, and that the result would be equitable given Norwegian oil and gas regulatory supervision.

The Arctic Council may have representation on the Joint Committee established in relation to any future JDZ in the Arctic Ocean region, primarily to supervise environmental regulations, and ensure coordination with environmental measures and emergency responses in the Arctic Ocean region.[281]

The JDZ may be made as a new agreement, a renegotiation of the Svalbard Treaty, or as a protocol to the Svalbard Treaty. Renegotiation of the Svalbard Treaty or a related Protocol is likely to be impractical, owing to the large number of state parties to the Svalbard Treaty. The more practical approach is likely to be made by a Norwegian declaration of a JDZ area consistent with the Svalbard Treaty. The JDZ structure should, however, offer a potential solution to the dispute and allow the development of oil and gas resources to proceed.

3.3.4 Central Arctic – Canada, Denmark (Greenland) and Russia

There is a potential overlap in the central Arctic Ocean between Canada, Denmark and Russia. The potential overlap is generally illustrated as arising from an equidistance line from their respective coasts extending beyond the North Pole, which would overlap the current submission made by Russia to the CLCS extending from the Russian coast to beyond the North Pole.[282] The potential

---

280 Article 8, Svalbard Treaty states in part that: 'Norway undertakes to provide for the territories specified in Article 1 mining regulations which, especially from the point of view of imposts, taxes or charges of any kind, and of general or particular labour conditions, shall exclude all privileges, monopolies or favours for the benefit of the State or of the nationals of any one of the High Contracting Parties, including Norway, and shall guarantee to the paid staff of all categories the remuneration and protection necessary for their physical, moral and intellectual welfare. Taxes, dues and duties levied shall be devoted exclusively to the said territories and shall not exceed what is required for the object in view.'

281 The Norwegian licencing regime allows foreign oil companies to explore and produce oil and gas in the Norwegian continental shelf and OCS. The proposed structure would also provide for complete Norwegian control as the licencing authority, consistent with the position taken by academic authorities discussed above. The JDZ terms would allow the taxing power to other states to benefit from the resources in the JDZ.

282 Donat Pharand, 'Canada's Arctic Jurisdiction in International Law' (1982–1983) 7 *Dalhousie Law Journal* 315, 318.

JDZ area, based on equidistance overlapping a Russian claim, is indicated on the IBRU map updated in 2015.[283] UNCLOS limits on the continental shelf may mean there are no overlaps, unless the Lomonosov and Mendeleev Ridges support an extended continental shelf, and this issue is therefore subject to CLCS review of the relevant geological data. The potential overlap is also subject to the CLCS recommendations on the revised Russian submission relating to the Lomonosov and Mendeleev Ridges, and the CLCS recommendations on the current Danish and Greenland Government submission and the anticipated Canadian final submission.[284]

There is currently no indication that Russia will not accept a future CLCS recommendation, and the Russian Arctic claim does not extend beyond the North Pole. Canada lodged the Preliminary Information concerning the outer limits of the continental shelf of Canada in the Arctic Ocean on 6 December 2013.[285] The Preliminary Information provided for a submission based on the Alpha and Lomonosov Ridges; however the Preliminary Information did not provide whether a submission would be made relating to any sea areas beyond the North Pole.[286] The Denmark and Greenland Government submission in December 2014 does extend beyond the North Pole and therefore overlaps the current Russian submission. There may be a potential need for a JDZ in the event that CLCS recommendations confirm that Canadian and Danish claims overlap the Russian claim and future maritime boundaries are not agreed.

One option to avoid the possibility of a deadlock between the Arctic states was to reach a boundary agreement before making a submission to the CLCS.[287] This was the position taken by Australia and New Zealand before their

283 Pratt (n. 63).

284 Weber (n. 267) at p. 662.

285 Commission on the Limits of the Continental Shelf, 'Preliminary Information concerning the outer limits of the continental shelf of Canada in the Arctic Ocean' (6 December 2013) at: http://www.un.org/depts/los/clcs_new/submissions_files/preliminary/can_pi_en.pdf (last accessed 4 April 2018). The filing of the preliminary information satisfied the time period in Article 4 of Annex II of the Convention, read in conjunction with decision SPLOS/183 adopted at the eighteenth meeting of States Parties to the Convention.

286 Ibid. The Preliminary Information stated:

"The continental margin of Canada in the Arctic Ocean is part of a morphologically continuous continental margin around the Canada Basin and along the Amundsen Basin. It comprises a number of seafloor elevations (Lomonosov Ridge and Alpha Ridge) and forms the submerged prolongation of the land mass of Canada. Throughout, the areas of continental shelf extend beyond 200 nautical miles from the territorial sea baselines of Canada and, on the Alpha and Lomonosov Ridges, beyond the 350 nautical mile constraint."

287 Monique Andree Allain, 'Canada's Claim To The Arctic: A Study In Overlapping Claims To The Outer Continental Shelf' (2011) 42 *Journal of Maritime Law and Commerce* 1.

respective CLCS submissions.[288] An alternative approach is to make a partial submission, allowing a submitting state with an extensive maritime or land dispute off its coast to put this aspect of its own claim 'into cold storage' until a future date, without being affected by the 10-year submission rule, while at the same time enabling a submission with respect to the state's continental shelf which does not overlap the claims of another state.[289] There is also a procedure based on paragraph 5 of Annex I of the Rules of Procedure, which allows the disputed areas of a submission to be examined with the prior consent of all coastal States involved.[290] Russia has yet to make public the contents of its initial submission and the recommendations of the CLCS and it is debatable whether or not Russia would change its approach and share the details of its claim with the other Arctic States.

The potential JDZs may be between Canada and Russia, and between Denmark (Greenland) and Russia. Canada and Denmark are coordinating a survey for the CLCS submissions,[291] and announced in 2012 that agreement had been reached in relation to the boundary in the Lincoln Sea.[292]

3.3.5 Central Arctic and Norwegian Sea – Three Zones under the Area Regime, UNCLOS Part XI

The Area regime is likely to apply to central areas in the Arctic Ocean, the central Bering Sea between the United States and Russia ('Central Bering Sea Doughnut Hole'), the Barents Sea ('Barents Sea Loophole'), and the Norwegian Sea ('Norwegian Sea Banana Hole').[293] The potential Arctic Ocean regions are

288 2004 Treaty between the Government of Australia and the Government of New Zealand establishing certain Exclusive Economic Zone and Continental Shelf Boundaries (2006) *ATS* 4.

289 Clive Symmons, 'The Irish Partial Submission to the Commission on the Limits of the Continental Shelf in 2005: A Precedent for Future Such Submissions in the Light of the "Disputed Areas" Procedures of the Commission?' (2006) 37 *Ocean Development and International Law* 3, at p. 4.

290 Alex G Oude Elferink, 'Submissions of Coastal States to the CLCS in Cases of Unresolved Land or Maritime Disputes', in Myron H Nordquist, John N Moore and Tomas H Heidar (eds), *Legal and Scientific Aspects of Continental Shelf Limits* (Martinus Nijhoff, Leiden/Boston: 2004) 263, at p. 268.

291 Allain (n. 291) at p. 1.

292 Government of Canada, Foreign Affairs and International Trade Canada, 'Canada and Kingdom of Denmark Reach Tentative Agreement on Lincoln Sea Boundary' Press Release (28 November 2012) at: https://www.canada.ca/en/news/archive/2012/11/canada-kingdom-denmark-reach-tentative-agreement-lincoln-sea-boundary.html (last accessed 4 April 2018).

293 Oude Elferink and Rothwell (n. 81) at p. 351.

shown as three unshaded areas in the IBRU Arctic Boundary Map;[294] however, this region may be larger if the CLCS does not recommend that a continental shelf can relate to the Lomonosov and Mendeleev Ridges.[295] The Area regime, as discussed, should, however, be viewed as a region allowing multilateral access, rather than a JDZ, particularly owing to the absence of special rights for adjacent states.

4 Joint Development Zones

4.1 *General Structure of JDZs and the BIICL Model Agreement*

JDZs have been introduced in several of the world's contested maritime regions where the states concerned have not been willing to be seen to surrender sovereignty in any boundary agreement. The more successful JDZs have allowed cooperation between the respective states and improved international relations. The potential advantages for JDZs in the Arctic Ocean region are therefore significant, because these regions are characterised by the potentially large number of overlapping claims.

A model JDZ Agreement and related research were issued by the British Institute of International and Comparative Law (BIICL). The research was edited by Hazel Fox, and published in *Joint Development of Offshore Oil and Gas* in 1989 (The BIICL Review).[296] A revised Model Agreement was published after further consultation in 1990 (the BIICL Model).[297] The purpose of the Model Agreement was to provide a general example for the shared pooling of the continental shelf jurisdiction which international law accords to the coastal state. The Model Agreement will not, by necessity, meet all the requirements for a specific JDZ agreement. Modifications will always be required to meet the needs of the respective state parties, and the specific circumstances of different regions. The BIICL review included analysis of multilateral development regimes, including the Area regime in UNCLOS Part XI.[298] The Articles of the BIICL Model included:

294 Pratt (n. 63).

295 This would potentially apply if these ridges are not classified as 'submarine elevations that are natural components of the continental margin,' and so would not support outer continental shelf claims.

296 Fox (n. 5) at p. 1.

297 Hazel Fox et al, *Joint Development of Offshore Oil and Gas, A Model Agreement for States for Joint Development with Explanatory Commentary* Vol 2 (British Institute of International and Comparative Law, London: 1990) 1.

298 Fox (n. 5) at p. 88.

- Article 3 – Principles of Joint Development
- Article 4 – Without Prejudice
- Articles 5 and 6 – Joint Commission
- Article 7 – Preparation of the Zone Plan
- Article 8 – Compliance and Enforcement
- Article 9 – Financial Terms of Development Contracts
- Article 10 – Approval of the Zone Plan
- Article 11 – Development Contracts
- Article 13 – Rights and Duties of Contractors
- Article 20 – Health and Safety
- Article 21 – Prevention of Pollution and Protection of the Marine Environment

The BIICL Model contained several alternative provisions: for example, the Article 11 Development Regime could use a concession/licence agreement which allows the contractor ownership of oil and gas and imposes tax and royalties, or a production-sharing contract regime which provides the oil-producing country with a direct portion of the oil and gas produced.[299] An important aspect of the BIICL Model was to provide for the Joint Commission to be the governing body of the JDZ in Articles 5 and 6, in order to provide a strong administration with separate legal authority to enable it to enter into contracts and conduct legal proceedings against third parties such as contractors. It was also significant that Article 21 of the BIICL Model provided the requirements to prevent pollution and protect the environment, which would be a critical clause, given the environmental risks in the Arctic Ocean region.

An analysis was made of the general structure of JDZ agreements by Ana E Bastida, Adaeze Ifesi-Okoye, Salim Mahmud et al, in 2007. The authors observed that existing joint petroleum development agreements show a wide variation in structure.[300] They identified six issues as being particularly important to the structure of JDZ agreements, as follows:

1. The sharing of resources from the JDZ was considered to be a key element to the success of the joint agreement. The perception that the basis for sharing is equitable and fundamental was essential to the ongoing relationship between the two states.[301]

299 See discussion of oil and gas fiscal regimes in John Abrahamson, *Tolley's International Taxation of Upstream Oil and Gas* 2nd ed (LexisNexis, London: 2017).

300 Ana E Bastida, Adaeze Ifesi-Okoye, Salim Mahmud et al, 'Cross-border unitization and joint development agreements: an international law perspective' (2006–2007) 29 *Houston Journal of International Law* 355, at p. 414.

301 Variations from equal sharing included the 1993 Senegal/Guinea-Bissau agreement (85:15 in favour of Senegal for petroleum resources), the 2001 Nigeria/São Tome and Principe

2. The management structure was generally of three types, comprising: a) the single-state model, with one state managing on behalf of both states: for example the 1958 Bahrain/Saudi Arabia agreement;[302] b) the two states/joint venture model, with each state nominating its own concessionaire, which enters into a joint venture with the concessionaire of the other state, including the Japan/South Korea JDZ;[303] and c) the Joint Authority model, with both states delegating power to a single authority responsible for supervision of petroleum activities, including the 1979/1990 Thailand/Malaysia agreements,[304] 1989 Australia/Indonesia Timor Gap Treaty,[305] 2001 Nigeria/São Tome and Principe agreement,[306] and 2002 Australia/Timor Leste Timor Sea Treaty.[307]
3. The agreements should state the applicable law, including the petroleum licensing regime, laws governing civil and criminal jurisdiction, and regulations governing health, safety and environmental issues. The petroleum licensing guidelines and other regulations may be specified in the agreement or may be established by the Joint Authority. The authors comment that criminal jurisdiction is generally based on the nationality of the

---

Agreement (60:40 in favour of Nigeria), and the 2002 Australia-Timor-Leste Timor Sea Treaty (90:10 in favour of Timor-Leste).

302 1958 Agreement Between the Kingdom of Saudi Arabia and the Government of Bahrain, 1993 *UNTS* 8 (Saudi Arabia/Bahrain Agreement).

303 1974 Agreement between Japan and the Republic of Korea concerning the Joint Development of the Southern part of the Continental Shelf adjacent to the Two Countries, 1225 *UNTS* 104 (Japan/Korea Agreement).

304 1979 Memorandum of Understanding between the Kingdom of Thailand and Malaysia on the Establishment of a Joint Authority for the Exploitation of the Resources of the Sea-Bed in a Defined Area of the Continental Shelf of the two countries in the Gulf of Thailand, reprinted in Charney and Alexander (n. 115) at p. 1099 (Thailand/Malaysia Agreement), and 1990 Agreement between the Government of Malaysia and the Government of the Kingdom of Thailand on the Constitution and Other Matters relating to the Establishment of the Malaysia-Thailand Joint Authority, at: https://cil.nus.edu.sg/wp-content/uploads/formidable/14/1990-Malaysia-Thailand-Joint-Authority.pdf (last accessed 2 March 2018).

305 1989 Treaty between Australia and the Republic of Indonesia in the Zone of Cooperation in an Area between the Indonesian Province of East Timor and Northern Australia, 1654 *UNTS* 106 (terminated on 2 April 2003) (Timor Gap Treaty).

306 2001 Treaty between the Federal Republic of Nigeria and the Democratic Republic of São Tome and Principe on the Joint Development of Petroleum and Other Resources, in respect of the Areas of the Exclusive Economic Zones of the Two States, United Nations – Delimitations Treaties Infobase, at: http://www.un.org/depts/los/LEGISLATIONANDTREATIES/PDFFILES/TREATIES/STP-NGA2001.PDF (last accessed 2 March 2018) (Nigeria/São Tome and Principe Treaty).

307 2002 Timor Sea Treaty, 2258 *UNTS* 3.

individual or by other agreement; however, jurisdiction may be applied by each state exercising jurisdiction on its side of an internal boundary line.

4. The agreement will either specify the basis for licensing the area of the JDZ, or will designate a Joint Authority to develop the rules for selecting contractors to undertake petroleum exploration and exploitation activities.
5. The agreement should provide the taxation regime, where: a) states may agree to adopt one state's taxation regime; b) apply the tax regime of the state that approved the contractor, or c) delegate the obligation to formulate fiscal terms to the Joint Authority. Taxation may alternatively apply at a discounted rate, where the contractor is liable for taxes only on a proportion of its profits to one state and the remainder to the other state.
6. The agreements provide for a dispute-resolution mechanism, which may include consultation, negotiation, conciliation, and binding commercial arbitration. The authors refer to the 2001 Nigeria/São Tome and Principe JDZ agreement,[308] which provides final dispute resolution as follows: a) settlement of disputes between the Joint Authority and private interests is subject to binding commercial arbitration under UNCITRAL rules; and b) disputes arising in the work of the Joint Authority or Joint Ministerial Council to an arbitral tribunal at the Permanent Court of Arbitration.

4.2 *JDZ Selected Examples*

A substantial number of JDZs have been established to date where states have not agreed a maritime boundary using an equidistance line. The various structures implemented under existing JDZs are broadly characterised as follows:

- Unitisation agreements, where states agree to share the revenues from an oil and gas field straddling a maritime boundary, such as the United Kingdom/Norway – Frigg Field Agreement in 1977;[309]

308 Nigeria/ São Tome Treaty (n. 310).

309 1976 Agreement Between the Government of the United Kingdom of Great Britain and Northern Ireland and the Government of the Kingdom of Norway relating to the Exploitation of the Frigg Field reservoir and the Transmission of Gas therefrom to the United Kingdom, 1098 *UNTS* 4.

- Preliminary or in-principle agreement, such as the China/Japan Agreement – East China Sea, 2008.[310] Such agreements have developed into effective JDZ areas, as in the Malaysia/Thailand – Joint Development Area, 1979;[311]
- Agreements with one state operating in the JDZ, with revenue sharing with the other state, such as the Malaysia/Vietnam Agreement in 1992;[312]
- Agreements with specific state provisions applying in the same JDZ zone, such as the Australia/Timor-Leste – Timor Sea Treaty in 2002;[313] and
- Agreements applying each state's laws on their respective side of an agreed maritime boundary within the JDZ area, as in the Iceland/Norway Agreement in the Jan Mayen Island area in 1981.[314]
- Multilateral agreements, where multiple states have access to resources, such as the Svalbard Treaty in 1920.[315] This can be considered as a related agreement, which, while allowing multilateral access to resources, less clearly falls within the standard definition of a JDZ.
- There are also examples of unsuccessful JDZ agreements which highlight the relationship between political circumstances and a successful JDZ. An example which should be considered in this respect is the Argentina/United Kingdom Joint Declaration to establish a JDZ in the South West Atlantic in 1995.[316]

---

310 Jiang Yu (Chinese Foreign Ministry), 'China, Japan reach principled consensus on East China Sea issue' Press Release (18 June 2009) at: http://www.china-embassy.org/eng/fyrth/t466632.htm (last accessed 4 April 2018).

311 1979 Memorandum of Understanding between the Kingdom of Thailand and Malaysia on the Establishment of a Joint Authority for the Exploitation of the Resources of the Sea-Bed in a Defined Area of the Continental Shelf of the two countries in the Gulf of Thailand, reprinted in Charney and Alexander (n. 115) at p. 1099.

312 1992 Memorandum of Understanding between Malaysia and the Socialist Republic of Vietnam for the Exploration and Exploitation of Petroleum in a Defined Area of the Continental Shelf Between the Two Countries, National University of Singapore – Centre for International Law (5 June 1992) at: https://cil.nus.edu.sg/wp-content/uploads/formidable/14/1992-MOU-between-Malaysia-and-Vietnam-for-the-Exploration-and-Exploitation-of-Petroleum.pdf (last accessed 2 March 2018).

313 2002 Timor Sea Treaty (n. 311).

314 1981 Agreement between Norway and Iceland on the Continental Shelf between Iceland and Jan Mayen, 2124 *UNTS* 262 (Norway/Iceland Agreement).

315 Svalbard Treaty (n. 212).

316 1995 Argentina/United Kingdom: Joint Declaration on Cooperation over Offshore Activities in the South West Atlantic, 35 *ILM* 301 (Argentina/United Kingdom Agreement).

The following is an analysis of the above specific JDZs established to date. These examples also show the potential adaptability of JDZ agreements to these circumstances.[317]

4.2.1 Unitisation Agreements – United Kingdom/Norway Agreement – Frigg Field Reservoir, 1976

In 1976, the United Kingdom and Norway agreed to a JDZ relating to the unitisation of a common petroleum deposit at the Frigg oilfield which straddled the continental shelf between the two countries.[318] The JDZ followed an earlier 1965 agreement on the delimitation of the continental shelf maritime boundary.[319] The JDZ provided that the proceeds derived from the field, and the costs of development, were to be allocated according to that portion of the deposit lying within the jurisdiction of the respective parties, generally resulting in a 60 per cent share to Norway, and 40 per cent share to the United Kingdom.[320] Accordingly, the JDZ was made for the purpose of effective exploitation of an oil and gas field where the boundary had previously been agreed, and is an example of the broader use of JDZs for economically efficient exploitation of oil and gas, rather than to share resources where a boundary cannot be agreed.[321] Unitisation agreements are therefore less relevant to the resolution of potential resource conflicts. Similar unitisation agreements in the North Sea include the Statfjord[322] and Murchison[323] agreements between

317 The list of JDZs is not exhaustive, and excludes JDZs which do not relate to significant ocean areas: for example, the limited area of the Ems estuary between the Netherlands and Germany.

318 1976 Agreement Between the Government of the United Kingdom of Great Britain and Northern Ireland and the Government of the Kingdom of Norway relating to the Exploitation of the Frigg Field reservoir and the Transmission of Gas therefrom to the United Kingdom, 1098 *UNTS* 4 (United Kingdom/Norway Agreement).

319 1965 Agreement between the United Kingdom and Norway relating to the delimitation of the Continental Shelf between the Two Countries, 551 *UNTS* 214.

320 University of Aberdeen – Politics Economics and Society, 'Capturing the Energy', (n.d.) at: http://www.capturing-the-energy.org.uk/frigg/ (last accessed 2 March 2018).

321 For reference on common petroleum deposits that straddle international boundaries see: William T Onorato, 'Apportionment of an International Common Petroleum Deposit' (1977) 26(2) *International and Comparative Law Quarterly* 324.

322 1979 Agreement between the Government of the Kingdom of Norway and the Government of the United Kingdom of Great Britain and Northern Ireland relating to the exploitation of the Statfjord Field Reservoirs and the offtake of petroleum therefrom, 1254 *UNTS* 379.

323 1979 Agreement between the Government of the Kingdom of Norway and the Government of the United Kingdom of Great Britain and Northern Ireland relating to the exploitation of the Murchison Field Reservoir and the offtake of petroleum therefrom, 1254 *UNTS* 173.

the United Kingdom and Norway, and the Markham agreement between the United Kingdom and the Netherlands.[324] The 1976 Agreement was made to conserve and make the best use of resources, prevent disputes between different parties, pool technical information, means and equipment, and reduce and rationalise the costs of exploitation.[325] The Agreement requires the resources of the Frigg Field to be apportioned by agreement on the basis of the proportions of reserves on the United Kingdom and Norwegian sides of the maritime boundary.[326] Activities were to be undertaken by licensees of both states under a single Unit Operator, which must be approved by both states.[327] The United Kingdom and Norway retain their jurisdiction over activities in their respective continental shelf areas.[328] Unitisation agreements therefore do not alter a maritime boundary but allow agreement on the sharing of resources between the respective states.

4.2.2 Preliminary Agreements – China/Japan Agreement – East China Sea, 2008 and Malaysia/Thailand – Joint Development Area, 1979

China and Japan agreed to a JDZ in June 2008 in the East China Sea.[329] The Agreement was released as a brief statement by Chinese Foreign Ministry Spokesperson Jiang Yu, with no detailed treaty, and therefore awaits a binding agreement to confirm the JDZ. The Japanese claim had been based on equidistance between baselines of the two states, whereas the Chinese claim had been based on natural prolongation of the Chinese coast. The JDZ straddles the median line; however, the majority of the JDZ is on the Japanese side of the median line.[330] Accordingly, the Agreement may be considered to be a compromise between the Japanese median line claim and the Chinese continental

324 1992 Agreement between the Government of the United Kingdom of Great Britain and Northern Ireland and the Netherlands relating to the exploitation of the Markham Field Reservoirs and the offtake of petroleum therefrom, 1731 *UNTS* 155.

325 Keith W Blinn et al, *International Petroleum Exploration and Exploitation Agreements* (The Barrows Company Inc, New York: 1986) 210.

326 Article 2(2), United Kingdom/Norway Agreement.

327 Article 5, United Kingdom/Norway Agreement.

328 Article 29(2), United Kingdom/Norway Agreement.

329 Yu (n. 314).

330 Clive Schofield and Ian Townsend-Gault, 'Choppy Waters Ahead in 'a sea of peace cooperation and friendship'? – Maritime Joint Development in the East China Sea', (Paper presented at the International Boundary Research Unit Conference, Durham, 2 April 2009) at: http://www.dur.ac.uk/ibru/conferences/sos/programme/2_april/track2_session4/#schofield (last accessed 4 April 2018).

shelf prolongation claim.[331] This is an 'in principle agreement' and, as at 2018, the detailed implementation remains to be developed. The JDZ area does not include the disputed Senkaku (Diaoyu) Islands. The development of the JDZ had been held up over a pre-existing field.[332] Subsequent events relating to the disputed Senkaku (Diaoyu) Islands have halted all movement toward formalising the 2008 consensus.[333]

The Agreement between Malaysia and Thailand was made in 1979,[334] and established a JDZ for a disputed area of approximately 7,250 square kilometres in the Gulf of Thailand, which was subject to continental shelf claims by both states.[335] The 1979 Agreement was followed by the 1990 Agreement on the constitution and other matters relating to the establishment of the Malaysia-Thailand Joint Authority.[336] David M Ong has commented that the 1990 Agreement was the culmination of over 10 years negotiation, and that the 1979 Agreement was essentially an expression of interest.[337] The maritime boundary dispute arose as Thailand claimed a continental shelf with the Thai island of Ko Losin as a base point, whereas Malaysia did not accept that the island could be used as a base point.[338] The two states were therefore

331 Reiji Yoshida and Shinichi Terada, 'Japan, China strike deal on gas fields ', *The Japan Times*, 19 June 2008, at: https://www.japantimes.co.jp/news/2008/06/19/national/japan-china-strike-deal-on-gas-fields/ (last accessed 3 April 2018).

332 James Manicom, 'China's Claims to an Extended Continental Shelf in the East China Sea: Meaning and Implications' (2009) 9(14) *China Brief* 9.

333 These events included the ramming of Japanese Coast Guard cutters by a Chinese fishing boat in 2010, and the subsequent arrest of the Chinese captain by Japan: James Manicom, 'Disputed Claims in the East China Sea', interview by Chris Acheson, The National Bureau of Asian Research, Seattle (25 July 2011) at: http://www.nbr.org/research/activity.aspx?id=159 (last accessed 4 April 2018).

334 1979 Memorandum of Understanding between the Kingdom of Thailand and Malaysia on the Establishment of a Joint Authority for the Exploitation of the Resources of the Sea-Bed in a Defined Area of the Continental Shelf of the two countries in the Gulf of Thailand, reprinted in Charney and Alexander (n. 115) at p. 1099 (Thailand/Malaysia Agreement).

335 Miyoshi and Schofield (n. 4) at p. 15.

336 1990 Agreement between the Government of Malaysia and the Government of the Kingdom of Thailand on the Constitution and Other Matters relating to the Establishment of the Malaysia-Thailand Joint Authority (30 May 1990) at: https://cil.nus.edu.sg/wp-content/uploads/formidable/14/1990-Malaysia-Thailand-Joint-Authority.pdf (last accessed 2 March 2018).

337 David M Ong, '1979 and 1990 Malaysia Thailand Joint Development Agreements: A Model for International Legal Cooperation in Common Offshore Petroleum Deposits?' (1999) 14(2) *International Journal of Marine and Coastal Law* 213.

338 Tara Davenport, 'Joint Development in Asia: Lessons for Sustainable Peace in the South China Sea', (Paper presented at 8th Asian Law Institute Conference, Kyushu, 26 and 27

not able to agree on a boundary, but wanted to provide for the joint exploitation of non-living resources of the seabed and subsoil. The 1979 Agreement provided that the maritime boundary and sovereign rights of the states are not prejudiced by the Agreement.[339] The Malaysia-Thailand Joint Authority was established with equal membership from each state, and exercises all powers necessary for the exploration and exploitation of the resources of the JDZ.[340] The Agreement requires the states and the Joint Authority to reach agreement in relation to resources which straddle the JDZ so that expenses and benefits are equitably shared.[341]

The JDZ is significant because of prior oil and gas licences in the JDZ area. The BIICL Review notes difficulties integrating the JDZ with exploration licences granted before the creation of the JDZ.[342] Ian Townsend-Gault has commented that Thailand was, however, willing to accept that the related fields were subject to the JDZ.[343] The JDZ is also significant because part of the area is claimed by Vietnam, referred to as the Tripartite Overlapping Claim Area. The JDZ is in current production, including 10 million barrels produced from Block A-18 of the Cakerawala oilfield in 2010.[344]

Preliminary agreements are therefore significant as a substantial step forwards in cooperation between states, and which can develop over time into productive JDZs.

4.2.3 Agreements with One State Operating in the JDZ – Malaysia/Vietnam Agreement, 1992

Malaysia and Vietnam agreed to establish a JDZ over a 'Defined Area' in 1992.[345] The Defined Area related to the overlapping claims of the two states, and the Agreement provided for exploration and exploitation of petroleum resources in the Defined Area 'pending final delimitation of the boundary lines of their continental shelves'.[346] The Defined Area has a length over 100 nautical miles,

May 2011) at: http://cil.nus.edu.sg/wp/wp-content/uploads/2011/06/TaraDavenport-ASLI-Joint-Development-as-a-tool-for-peace-4-April-2011–v2.pdf (last accessed 4 April 2018).

339 Article 5, Thailand/Malaysia Agreement.

340 Articles 3(3) and 3(4), Thailand/Malaysia Agreement.

341 Article 3(3), Thailand/Malaysia Agreement.

342 Fox et al (n. 5) at p. 62. Thailand granted the concessions to Triton Petroleum Corporation ('Triton').

343 Ian Townsend-Gault, 'The Impact of a Joint Development Zone on Previously Granted Interests', in Fox (n. 301) at p. 106.

344 Malaysia Thailand Joint Authority, 'Chronicle' (n.d.) at: https://www.mtja.org/chronicle.php (last accessed 2 March 2018).

345 Malaysia/Vietnam Agreement (n. 316).

346 Article 2(1), Malaysia/Vietnam Agreement (n. 316).

and a width less than 10 nautical miles.[347] The Area runs in a south-east to north-west direction between the 1971 continental shelf claim of Vietnam and the 1979 continental shelf claim of Malaysia, with the north-west boundary adjoining the boundary of the Thailand/Malaysia 1979 JDZ. The Malaysian boundary claim relating to this area was made on the basis of giving effect to Redang Island without adjustment for Vietnamese offshore islands. The Vietnamese claim was made on the basis of an equidistance line between the Malaysian and Vietnamese mainlands without adjustment for offshore islands.[348] A related commercial agreement between the Malaysian state oil company Petronas[349] and the Vietnamese state oil company Petrovietnam[350] was made in 1993 to establish the Co-ordination Committee to implement the 1992 Agreement.

The Agreement provided that Malaysia and Vietnam would nominate Petronas and Petrovietnam, respectively, to undertake operations in the Defined Area.[351] Miyoshi comments that 'as Vietnam was not well prepared for the scheme of co-operation with Malaysia, Petronas was to carry out all joint development operations and provide Petrovietnam with an equal share of the net revenue.'[352] Malaysia had entered into a continuance of a 1989 Production Sharing Contract (PSC) signed by Petronas; however, this was modified to add Petrovietnam as a party.[353] The related tax returns are prepared under Malaysian tax rules. Half the tax is then paid to Malaysia, and half paid to Vietnam.[354] The first petroleum was produced from the Bunga Kekwa field in the Defined Zone in 1997.[355]

These agreements allow development where one state is able to lead the development effort while retaining equal sharing of the resources of the JDZ region.

---

347 Miyoshi and Schofield (n. 4) at p. 15.

348 Charney and Alexander (n. 190) at p. 2335.

349 Petroliam Nasional Berhad (Petronas).

350 Petrovietnam Oil and Gas Group (Petrovietnam).

351 Article 3, Malaysia/Vietnam Agreement (n. 316).

352 Masahiro Miyoshi, 'Seabed Petroleum in the East China Sea: Law of the Sea Issues and the Prospects for Joint Development' (n.d.) 9, at: https://www.wilsoncenter.org/sites/default/files/Miyoshi_Masahiro.pdf (last accessed 2 March 2018).

353 Lan-Anh T Nguyen, 'Joint Development between Malaysia and Vietnam' (n.d.) at: https://cil.nus.edu.sg/wp-content/uploads/2011/06/Session-5-Lan-Anh-Joint-development-between-Malaysia-Vietnam-pdf.pdf (last accessed 2 March 2018).

354 This arrangement differs from the Malaysia/Thailand JDZ, where tax is determined in separate tax returns under each state's tax rules, with half the tax calculated then paid to the respective government.

355 Nguyen (n. 357).

4.2.4 Agreements with Specific State Provisions Applying in the Same JDZ – Australia/Timor-Leste – Timor Sea Treaty, 2002

The Agreement between Australia and Timor-Leste concerns oil and gas in an area of the Timor Sea between the two states (Timor Sea Treaty). The Agreement is based on the earlier Timor Gap Treaty made between Australia and Indonesia in the same region).[356] In 2018 the parties reached agreement on a new Timor Sea Treaty which upon entry into force will terminate the operation of the 2002 Timor Sea Treaty.[357] Australia's claim in 2002 was based on the natural prolongation of the continental shelf in the Timor Sea. The Timor-Leste claim was based on equidistance between the respective coastlines.[358] Clive Schofield has commented that Australia withdrew from the maritime boundary jurisdiction of the ICJ and ITLOS in March 2002, two months prior to independence of Timor-Leste.[359] The Timor Sea Treaty established a Joint Petroleum Development Area (JPDA) with joint control of exploration and exploitation.[360] The JPDA was equivalent to the shared 'Area A' of the prior Australia and Indonesia Timor Gap Treaty.[361] Petroleum production from the JPDA was shared 90 per cent to Timor-Leste and 10 per cent to Australia.[362] This ratio was based on Australian recognition of the development needs of Timor-Leste.[363] The sovereignty of either country in respect of the JPDA was not affected by the Treaty, which provides that it shall not prejudice the position of either state in permanent continental shelf delimitation.[364]

---

356 Timor Gap Treaty (n. 309).

357 2018 Treaty Between Australia and the Democratic Republic of Timor-Leste Establishing Their Maritime Boundaries in the Timor Sea (Timor Sea Treaty) at: http://dfat.gov.au/geo/timor-leste/Documents/treaty-maritime-arrangements-australia-timor-leste.pdf (last accessed 3 April 2018).

358 Mark Valencia and Masahiro Miyoshi, 'Southeast Asian Seas: Joint Development of Hydrocarbons in Overlapping Claim Areas' (1996) 16 *Ocean Development and International Law* 211, at p. 229.

359 Clive Schofield, 'Minding the Gap: The Australia-East Timor Treaty on Certain Maritime Arrangements in the Timor Sea (CMATS)' (2007) 22(2) *International Journal of Marine and Coastal Law* 201.

360 Article 3 (a), Timor Sea Treaty.

361 Australian Government, 'Timor Gap Treaty (Transitional Arrangements) Bill 2000', Bills Digest No 133 1999–2000, at: https://www.aph.gov.au/Parliamentary_Business/Bills_Legislation/bd/Bd9900/2000bd133 (last accessed 3 April 2018).

362 Article 4 (a), Timor Sea Treaty.

363 Ibid. The Timor Gap Treaty shared petroleum resources on the basis of 50 per cent to each state within a central sector of the JDZ.

364 Article 2(b), Timor Sea Treaty.

The provisions require the unitisation of reservoirs of petroleum that extend across the boundary of the JPDA.[365]

There were several important changes between the terms of the Timor Sea Treaty and the prior Timor Gap Treaty.[366] These changes included that Timor-Leste derived 90 per cent of the income from the JPDA, and the Joint Commission has two members appointed by Timor-Leste, and Australia appoints one member, giving Timor-Leste control of measures including contracts with third parties for oil and gas development. The Sunrise International Unitisation Agreement (Sunrise IUA) concerns a related issue for the Sunrise and Troubadour offshore oil and gas fields, known as the 'Greater Sunrise' field, which straddled the JPDA, extending to the east beyond the JPDA area. Australia and Timor-Leste signed the Sunrise IUA in 2003.[367] The Agreement was ratified by Timor-Leste in 2007 at the same time as the Treaty on Certain Maritime Arrangements in the Timor Sea (CMATS).[368] The CMATS Treaty modified the revenue sharing from the Greater Sunrise field to 50 per cent to both states. Timor Leste referred the underlying international boundary issue to compulsory conciliation under UNCLOS Annex V on 11 April 2016. The Conciliation Commission established under the auspices of the Permanent Court of Arbitration held that it was competent to hear the dispute on 19 September 2016.[369]

Extensive oil and gas operations are underway in the JDZ, and a summary of the petroleum-production profit-sharing data between Timor-Leste and

---

365 Article 9, Timor Sea Treaty. These reservoirs were treated as a single entity for management and development purposes.

366 Gillian Triggs and Dean Bialek, 'The New Timor Sea Treaty and Interim Arrangements for Joint Development of Petroleum resources of the Timor Gap' (2002) 3 *Melbourne Journal of International Law* 322.

367 2003 Agreement between the Government of Australia and the Government of the Democratic Republic of Timor-Leste relating to the Unitisation of the Sunrise and Troubadour Fields [2007] *ATS* 11 (Australia/Timor-Leste – Sunrise IUA). The Agreement deemed 20.1 per cent of the resources of the Greater Sunrise field to be within the JPDA, with 90 per cent of that income to go to Timor-Leste under the Timor Sea Treaty. Timor-Leste would therefore have received 18.1 per cent of revenue from the field.

368 2006 Treaty between Australia and the Democratic Republic of Timor-Leste on Certain Maritime Arrangements in the Timor Sea [2007] *ATS* 12 (Australia/Timor-Leste – CMATS Treaty).

369 *In the Matter of a Conciliation before a Conciliation Commission Constituted Under Annex V to the 1982 United Nations Convention on the Law of the Sea between the Democratic Republic of Timor-Leste and the Commonwealth of Australia*, PCA Case No 2016–10, Decision on Australia's Objections to Competence of 19 September 2016, at: https://pcacases.com/web/sendAttach/1921 (last accessed 1 March 2018).

Australia during the time frame of December 2004 through July 2009 revenue summaries were published in July 2009.[370]

The agreement is an example of allowing state laws within the JDZ region, which can be considered as retaining certain sovereign powers for the respective states.

4.2.5 Agreements Applying Each State's Laws on Their Respective Side of Agreed Boundary – Iceland/Norway Agreement – Jan Mayen Island Area, 1981

Iceland and Norway entered into an Agreement in relation to the Continental Shelf in 1981,[371] which included a JDZ area.[372] The Agreement followed agreements on the EEZ in 1980 and 1981,[373] which generally provided a 200-nautical-mile EEZ to Iceland, based on Iceland's size relative to Norway's Jan Mayen Island, rather than being based on equidistance.[374] The continental shelf boundary between Iceland and the Norwegian island of Jan Mayen was referred to a Conciliation Commission.[375] The Commission did not recommend a new continental shelf boundary, but instead recommended that the same line as the EEZ boundary should apply, together with a JDZ overlapping the EEZ boundary.[376]

Iceland and Norway entered into the Agreement in 1981,[377] establishing a JDZ based on the recommendations of the Conciliation Commission. The Agreement provided that the continental shelf boundary is the same as the EEZ; accordingly, the Agreement does establish state sovereignty and a final boundary for competing continental shelf claims.[378] The JDZ extends approximately 12,720 square kilometres on the Icelandic side of the maritime boundary, and

370 Revenue Watch Institute, *Timor Sea Designated Authority First Tranche Petroleum and Profit Oil* (2009) at: http://www.revenuewatch.org/training/resource_center/timor-sea-designated-authority-first-tranche-petroleum-and-profit oil (last accessed 4 April 2018).

371 1981 Agreement between Norway and Iceland on the Continental Shelf between Iceland and Jan Mayen, 2124 *UNTS* 262 (Norway/Iceland Agreement).

372 ArcticEcon, 'Iceland's New Era of Offshore Exploration' (14 January 2013) at: https://arcticecon.wordpress.com/category/iceland/ (last accessed 3 April 2018).

373 Norway/Iceland Agreement.

374 Oude Elferink (n. 113) at p. 183.

375 Miyoshi and Schofield (n. 4) at p. 34. Iceland claimed a continental shelf based on its coast, and Norway claimed a continental shelf based on the Norwegian Jan Mayen Island.

376 Report and Recommendation to the Governments of Iceland and Norway of the Conciliation Commission on the Continental Shelf Area between Iceland and Jan Mayen (1981) 20 *ILM* 825.

377 Norway/Iceland Agreement.

378 Article 1, Norway/Iceland Agreement.

32,750 square kilometres on the Norwegian side. The JDZ provides that a 25 per cent share in petroleum activities from the JDZ inside the boundary of one state shall go to the other state.[379] The Agreement provides for the unitisation of deposits which straddle the JDZ and either country's OCS outside the JDZ.[380]

This form of agreement provides a clear jurisdiction because it provides which state laws will apply within two parts of the JDZ region. The agreement is also significant as an example of a bilateral JDZ in the Arctic Ocean region.

4.2.6 Multilateral Agreements Where Multiple States Have Access to Resources – Svalbard Treaty, 1920

The Svalbard Treaty[381] as discussed above is an example where multiple states have access to resources. The Treaty should, however, be considered as a form of sister agreement to a JDZ, rather than a JDZ more formally defined. The Treaty allows multilateral access to resources, and does not provide for the pooling of state claims to resources. The Treaty lacks the detailed terms for management of the zone generally required under the definition of a JDZ.

Norway adopted straight baselines in 2001 around the Svalbard Islands, and adopted a 12-nautical-mile territorial sea around the Islands in 2003.[382] Norway declared a 200-nautical-mile continental shelf in 1985 which applied to mainland and island coasts, and announced that it was opening an area to oil and gas exploration in the continental shelf around the Islands. The Soviet Union and the United Kingdom protested the declaration. No oil or gas concessions had been granted in this area as at December 2014. The agreement is, however, an example where multiple state claims to resources can be resolved whilst being combined with the advantages where one state has sovereignty to enforce its legal provisions in the maritime region. The agreement is also significant as to whether it relates to the resources of the Svalbard continental shelf.

379 Articles 5 and 7, Norway/Iceland Agreement. Each state is required to share the costs of surveys on the same percentage basis.

380 Article 8, Norway/Iceland Agreement.

381 Article 1, Svalbard Treaty.

382 Caracciolo (n. 220).

4.2.7 Currently Unsuccessful Agreements – Argentina/United Kingdom Joint Declaration to Establish a JDZ in the South West Atlantic, 1995

Argentina and the United Kingdom issued a Joint Declaration to establish a JDZ in the South West Atlantic in 1995.[383] The JDZ was to the south-west of the Falkland (Malvinas) Islands[384] and related regions.[385] The JDZ agreement was, however, cancelled by Argentina in 2007,[386] and the JDZ is a significant example of how JDZ agreements are subject to the political climate in the countries concerned.

Both the United Kingdom and Argentina claim sovereignty over the Falkland Islands. The Argentine claim is based on succession to the rights of Spain, territorial integrity, continental contiguity, occupation, and protest against the United Kingdom's claim.[387] The United Kingdom's claim is based on discovery, occupation and administration.[388] The Falkland Islands were the location of an armed conflict between the United Kingdom and Argentina in 1982. Argentina invaded the Islands in 1982, and the United Kingdom recaptured the Islands later in that year.[389] In November 1986 the United Kingdom declared a 200-nautical-mile continental shelf, which was implemented in November 1991 by the Governor of the Falklands in a proclamation establishing a 400,000-square-kilometre continental shelf claim.[390] Diplomatic relations between Argentina and the United Kingdom resumed in 1989 following the restoration of democracy in Argentina. Both countries continue to claim

---

383 1995 Argentina/United Kingdom: Joint Declaration on Cooperation over Offshore Activities in the South West Atlantic, 35 *ILM* 301 (Argentina/United Kingdom Agreement).

384 Patrick Armstrong and Vivian Forbes, 'The Falkland Islands and their Adjacent Maritime Area' (1995) 2(3) *IBRU Maritime Briefing* 27.

385 International Boundaries Research Unit (University of Durham), 'Argentina and UK claims to maritime jurisdiction in the South Atlantic and Southern Oceans' (n.d.) at: https://www.dur.ac.uk/ibru/resources/south_atlantic/ (last accessed 4 April 2018).

386 'Argentina Ends Falklands Oil Deal', *BBC News* (28 March 2007) at: http://news.bbc.co.uk/2/hi/americas/6501693.stm (last accessed 4 April 2018).

387 Ministry of Foreign Affairs, Argentine Republic, '*The Question of the Malvinas Islands*' (2012) at: www.consuladoargentinoenmiami.org/userfiles/Folleto_CuestionMalvinas_INGLES.pdf (last accessed 2 March 2018).

388 Falkland Islands Continental Shelf Proclamation, 17 February 1997, No.1 of 1991, at: https://www.ecolex.org/details/legislation/proclamation-no-1-of-1991-continental-shelf-lex-faoc001150/ (last accessed 2 March 2018).

389 Malcolm N Shaw, *International Law* 6th ed (Cambridge University Press, Cambridge: 2008) 532.

390 Falkland Islands Continental Shelf Proclamation (n. 392).

sovereignty over the Falkland Islands and the continental shelf;[391] however, improved relations made possible the Joint Declaration in 1995 establishing a Zone of Cooperation of about 20,000 square kilometres extending on both sides of the Falklands continental shelf boundary. The Declaration provided that exploration and exploitation of hydrocarbons by the offshore oil and gas industry was to be carried out in accordance with sound commercial principles and good oil field practice, drawing upon the Governments' experience both in the South West Atlantic and in the North Sea.[392] The Declaration established a Joint Commission, composed of delegations from both countries.[393] The Joint Commission was responsible for the administration of the JDZ.[394] The Declaration provided for coordinated activities in up to 6 tranches of about 3,500 square kilometres.[395] The Declaration provided that it did not change the respective positions of Argentina or the United Kingdom in respect of sovereignty or territorial and maritime jurisdiction.[396]

The United Kingdom made a partial submission to the CLCS in respect of an OCS for the Falkland Islands, South Georgia and the South Sandwich Islands on 11 May 2009.[397] The submission extends to an ocean area south of 60°S, within the area subject to the 1959 Antarctic Treaty. The submission noted overlapping claims, and requested that the 'partial submission and the recommendations of the Commission made in respect of it will not prejudice matters relating to the delimitation of boundaries.'[398] Argentina made a continental shelf submission to the CLCS including the Southern Ocean on 21 April 2009.[399] The Argentine submission included the continental shelf extending

391 TW Walde and Andrew McHardy, 'Introductory Note, Argentina – United Kingdom: Joint Declaration on Cooperation over Offshore Activities in the South West Atlantic' (1996) 35 *ILM* 301.

392 Article 2, Argentina/United Kingdom Agreement.

393 Article 2(a), Argentina/United Kingdom Agreement.

394 Article 4(b), Argentina/United Kingdom Agreement.

395 Article 2(b), Argentina/United Kingdom Agreement.

396 Article 1, Argentina/United Kingdom Agreement.

397 Commission on the Limits of the Continental Shelf, 'United Kingdom Submission in respect of the Falkland Islands, and of South Georgia and the South Sandwich Islands' (11 May 2009) at: http://www.un.org/Depts/los/clcs_new/submissions_files/submission_gbr_45_2009.htm (last accessed 4 April 2018).

398 Ibid., at p. 3. The United Kingdom's submission stated: '... the UK wishes to inform the Commission that, in its view, this partial submission and the recommendations of the Commission made in respect of it will not prejudice matters relating to the delimitation of boundaries between the UK and any other State.'

399 Commission on the Limits of the Continental Shelf, 'Outer Limits of the Continental Shelf – Argentine Submission' (21 April 2009) at: https://www.un.org/depts/los/clcs_new/submissions_files/submission_arg_25_2009.htm (last accessed 4 April 2018).

from the Falklands Islands in addition to the continental shelf extending from Antarctic territory.

The Falkland Islands region is currently of interest for potential offshore oil and gas. The Falkland Oil and Gas Limited had received exploration permits to the south and south-east of the Falkland Islands. These permits are adjacent to the prior JDZ area to the south-west of the Islands, but do not extend into that JDA area.[400]

The agreement is significant example of a currently unsuccessful JDZ, and emphasises the importance of favourable political circumstances for a successful JDZ. The agreement may also potentially develop into the basis of a successful JDZ in the future.

4.3 *Similarities to Potential Arctic JDZs*

The existing JDZs are listed in Table 3, which includes the geographical circumstances of the JDZ, together with a code identifying the basis on which one or more parties did not accept a boundary based on equidistance.

The key point is that existing JDZs have been used to allow cooperative development in a variety of dispute circumstances, which include archipelagic claims, coastal length, historical circumstances, prior treaty, island effects and sovereignty, land sovereignty, multilateral claims, prolongation of continental shelf, and unitising oil or gas fields.

Several of the Arctic Ocean maritime boundary disputes have similar general characteristics to previous or current JDZs. These are:

- The issue of unilateral claims was addressed in the Svalbard Treaty, the issue of historical treaties was addressed in Guinea-Bissau/Senegal JDZ,[401]
- the issue of claims based on the extension of the physical continental shelf compared to equidistance was addressed in the Australia/Timor-Leste JDZ,[402]
- the issue of disputed land sovereignty was addressed in the Malaysia/Brunei JDZ,[403]
- the issue of disputed island sovereignty was addressed in the Qatar/Abu Dhabi JDZ,[404] and

400 Falkland Oil and Gas Limited, 'Investor Presentation' (November 2011) at: http://ww7.investorrelations.co.uk/fogl/en/Investors/results (last accessed 2 March 2018), and Falkland Islands Department of Mineral Resources, 'Exploration History' (n.d.) at: http://www.fig.gov.fk/minerals/exploration/historical-activity (last accessed 2 March 2018).

401 Guinea-Bissau and Senegal Agreement.

402 Timor Sea Treaty.

403 Malaysia/Brunei JDZ (n. 431).

404 Qatar/Abu Dhabi Agreement (n. 409).

TABLE 3 Current JDZ examples and related geographical circumstances

	Agreement	Geographical Circumstances	Code
1.	Svalbard Treaty, 1920,[a]	Multilateral access to resources of Svalbard Islands under Svalbard Treaty 1920	H, M, IS
2.	Saudi Arabia/Kuwait Neutral Zone, 1922,[b] Agreement, 1965,[c]	Adjoining states	H
3.	Saudi Arabia/Bahrain, 1958,[d]	Coastline and Island	IE
4.	Qatar/Abu Dhabi, 1969,[e]	Opposite coasts	IS
5.	Iran/Sharjah (United Arab Emirates), 1971,[f]	Opposite coasts	IS
6.	France/Spain, Bay of Biscay, 1974,[g]	Adjoining coasts, France mid-point of ocean trough, Spain equidistance, effectively sharing potential fields	PCS, U
7.	Sudan/Saudi Arabia – Common Zone, 1974,[h]	Opposite coasts	PCS
8.	Japan/Korea, 1974,[i]	Opposite coasts, Japan equidistance, Korea, continental shelf	PCS
9.	United Kingdom/Norway – Frigg Field, 1977,[j]	Included as a unitisation example, boundary previously agreed. Opposite coasts, effectively sharing field	U
10.	Malaysia/Thailand – Joint Development Area, 1979,[k] and 1990,[l]	Adjoining coasts, Thailand claimed island as base for continental shelf	IE
11.	Iceland/Norway – Jan Mayen Island Treaty Area, 1981,[m]	Island continental shelf	IE
12.	Cambodia/Vietnam Agreement, 1982,[n]	Adjoining coats, issue of Cambodian islands affecting equidistance	IE
13.	Tunisia/Libya Agreements, 1988,[o]	Adjoining coasts following ICJ decision using equitable principles	CL

TABLE 3 Current JDZ examples and related geographical circumstances (*cont.*)

	Agreement	Geographical Circumstances	Code
14.	Australia/Indonesia – Timor Gap Treaty, 1989,[p]	Opposite coasts, Australia, prolongation continental shelf, Indonesia, equidistance	PCS
15.	Malaysia/Vietnam, 1992,[q]	Opposite coasts, Vietnam equidistance on mainlands, Malaysia equidistance using Redang Island	IE
16.	Guinea-Bissau/Senegal, 1993,[r]	Adjacent coasts, 1960 agreement between colonial powers France and Portugal compared to equidistance	H
17.	Colombia/Jamaica, 1993,[s]	Claimed archipelagic baseline and opposite coast	A
18.	United Kingdom/Argentina Joint Declaration South West Atlantic, 1995,[t]	Island sovereignty issue	IS
19.	Nigeria/São Tome and Principe, 2001,[u]	Island and opposite coast, Nigeria, length respective coasts, São Tome archipelagic baseline,	CL
20.	Thailand/Cambodia MOU, 2001,[v]	Effect to be given to Thailand's Ko Kut Island, interpretation of 1907 France Siamese treaty	H, IE
21.	Australia/Timor-Leste – Timor Sea Treaty, 2002,[w] Sunrise IUA, 2003,[x] CMATS, 2007,[y]	Opposite coasts, Australia, prolongation continental shelf, Timor-Leste, equidistance	PCS, U
22.	China/Japan Agreement – East China Sea, 2008,[z]	China on natural prolongation continental shelf, Japan, equidistance	PCS
23.	Malaysia/Agreement, 2009,[aa]	Adjoining coasts	LS

TABLE 3 Current JDZ examples and related geographical circumstances (*cont.*)

Code	Basis for claims other than equidistance
A	Archipelago claim
CL	Coast length
H	Historical circumstances or prior treaty
IE	Island effects
IS	Island sovereignty
LS	Land sovereignty
M	Multilateral claims
PCS	Prolongation of continental shelf
U	Unitising oil or gas field

a Svalbard Treaty (n. 212).

b Agreement concerning the boundary between Nejd and Kuwait, opened for signature 2 December 1922, 1750 *UNTS* 533 (entered into force 2 December 1922) (Uqair Convention).

c Kuwait-Saudi Arabia Neutral Zone Agreement, opened for signature 7 July 1965, (1966) 60 *American Journal of International Law* 744 (entered into force 7 July 1965) (translated by Sayed M. Hosni) (Saudi Arabia/Kuwait Agreement).

d Agreement Between the Kingdom of Saudi Arabia and the Government of Bahrain, 22 February 1958, 1993 *UNTS* 8 (entered into force 22 February 1958) (Saudi Arabia/Bahrain Agreement).

e 1969 Agreement Concerning Settlement of Offshore Boundaries and Ownership of Islands Between Qatar and Abu Dhabi, 2402 *UNTS* 54 (Qatar/Abu Dhabi Agreement).

f Memorandum of Understanding' between Iran and Sharjah (29 November 1971) at: http://www.parstimes.com/history/iran_sharjah.html (last accessed 1 March 2018) (Iran/Sharjah MOU).

g Convention Between the Government of the French Republic and the Government of the Spanish State on the Delimitation of the Continental Shelves of the Two States in the Bay of Biscay, 29 January 1974, 996 *UNTS* 345 (entered into force 29 January 1974) (France/Spain Agreement).

h Agreement Between Sudan and Saudi Arabia Relating to the Joint Exploitation of the Natural Resources of the Seabed and Subsoil of the Common Zone, 16 May 1974, 952 *UNTS* 198 (entered into force 16 May 1974) (Sudan/Saudi Arabia Agreement).

i Agreement between Japan and the Republic of Korea concerning the Joint Development of the Southern part of the Continental Shelf adjacent to the Two Countries, 30 January 1974, 1225 *UNTS* 104 (entered into force 22 June 1978) (Japan/Korea Agreement).

j Agreement Between the Government of the United Kingdom of Great Britain and Northern Ireland and the Government of the Kingdom of Norway relating to the Exploitation of the Frigg Field reservoir and the Transmission of Gas therefrom to the United Kingdom, 10 May 1976, 1098 *UNTS* 4 (entered into force 22 July 1977) (United Kingdom/Norway Agreement).

k Memorandum of Understanding between the Kingdom of Thailand and Malaysia on the Establishment of a Joint Authority for the Exploitation of the Resources of the Sea-Bed in a Defined Area of the Continental Shelf of the two countries in the Gulf of Thailand, 21 September 1979, reprinted in Jonathan I Charney and Lewis M Alexander (eds), *International Maritime Boundaries* Vol 1 (Martinus Nijhoff, Dordrecht/Boston: 1993) 1099 (entered into force 24 October 1979) (Thailand/Malaysia Agreement).

l 1990 Agreement between Malaysia and Thailand on the constitution and other matters relating to the establishment of the Malaysia-Thailand Joint Authority.

m Agreement between Norway and Iceland on the Continental Shelf between Iceland and Jan Mayen, signed 22 October 1981, 2124 *UNTS* 262 (entered into force 2 June 1982) (Norway/Iceland Agreement).

n Agreement on Historic Waters of Vietnam and Kampuchea, signed 7 July 1982, reproduced in Jonathan I Charney and Lewis M Alexander (eds), *International Maritime Boundaries* Vol 3 (Martinus Nijhoff, Dordrecht/Boston: 1998) 2364 (Vietnam/Cambodia Agreement).

o Agreement between President Ben Ali of Tunisia and Colonel Qadhafi of the Libyan Arab Jamahiriya relating to the El Bouri Field, 4 September 1988 (Not publicly released), analysed in Miyoshi (n. 4) (Libya/Tunisia Agreements).

p Timor Gap Treaty (n. 309).

q Memorandum of Understanding between Malaysia and the Socialist Republic of Vietnam for the Exploration and Exploitation of Petroleum in a Defined Area of the Continental Shelf Between the Two Countries, 5 June 1992 (entered into force 4 June 1993) at: https://cil.nus.edu.sg/wp-content/uploads/formidable/14/1992-MOU-between-Malaysia-and-Vietnam-for-the-Exploration-and-Exploitation-of-Petroleum.pdf (last accessed 3 April 2018) (Malaysia/Vietnam Agreement).

r 1993 Agreement on Management and Cooperation between the Government of the Republic of Guinea-Bissau and the Government of the Republic of Senegal, 1903 *UNTS* 64 (Guinea-Bissau and Senegal Agreement).

s Maritime Delimitation Treaty between Jamaica and the Republic of Colombia, 12 November 1993, 1776 *UNTS* 17 (entered into force 14 March 1994) (Jamaica/Colombia Treaty).

t Argentina/United Kingdom Joint Declaration (n. 320).

u Treaty between the Federal Republic of Nigeria and the Democratic Republic of São Tome and Principe on the Joint Development of Petroleum and Other Resources, in respect of the Areas of the Exclusive Economic Zones of the Two States, 21 February 2001 (entered into force 21 February 2001) at: http://www.un.org/depts/los/legislationandtreaties/pdffiles/treaties/STP-NGA2001.PDF (last accessed 3 April 2018) (Nigeria/São Tome and Principe Agreement).

v Memorandum of Understanding between the Royal Thai Government and the Royal Government of Cambodia regarding the Area of their Overlapping Maritime Claims to the Continental Shelf, 18 June 2001, discussed in David A Colson and Robert W Smith (eds) *International Maritime Boundaries* Vol 5 (Martinus Nijhoff, Leiden/Boston: 2005) at p. 3735 (Thailand/Cambodia Agreement).

w Timor Sea Treaty (n. 311).

x Australia/Timor-Leste – Sunrise IUA.

y Australia/Timor-Leste – CMATS Treaty.

z Yu (n. 314).

aa 2009 Exchange of Letters between Malaysia and Brunei Darussalam, (not publicly released), referred to in Jeffrey J Smith, 'Brunei and Malaysia resolve outstanding maritime boundary issues' [2010] 1 *Law of the Sea Reports*, at: https://www.peacepalacelibrary.nl/ebooks/files/353834688.pdf (last accessed 2 March 2018) (Malaysia/Brunei JDZ), and International Boundaries Research Unit (University of Durham), 'Details Emerge of the 2009 Brunei-Malaysia Maritime Agreement' (2010) at: https://www.dur.ac.uk/ibru/news/boundary_news/?itemno=10047&rehref=%2Fibru%2Fnews%2F&resubj=Boundary+news+Headlines (last accessed 2 March 2018).

– the effect to be given to islands was addressed in the Malaysia/Vietnam JDZ.[405]

In summary, there have been a significant number of JDZs agreed between states, and there is a common characteristic of the adaptability of these agreements to the different geographical and historical circumstances which gave rise to maritime boundary disputes.

5 Joint Development in the Arctic – Implementation Issues

5.1 *Political* Changes

5.1.1 Autonomy or Independence

Changes in government may have a significant influence on the prospects for oil and gas development, including the priority given to oil and gas activities. A new government in Greenland halted new offshore drilling licences in 2013.[406] The reasons for the halt included concerns that the oil and gas industry may adversely affect traditional hunting and fishing activities.[407] Full independence of Greenland may increase the priority given to conservation and preservation of the environment.

There is also a trend in other regions towards increased autonomy and control over resources. Canada's Nunavut regional government has a consultative role on oil and gas development.[408] For example: the '2012–2013 Call For Nominations – Arctic Islands of Nunavut', issued in 2013, was an invitation to bid for exploration licences in potential gas fields related to Crown lands within the Nunavut Settlement Area.[409] Canada's Northwest Territories became responsible for managing the land within its boundaries and granting oil and gas rights under the 2013 Northwest Territories Land and Resources

405 Malaysia /Vietnam Agreement (n. 316).

406 'Greenland halts new oil drilling licences', *The Guardian* (27 March 2013), at: http://www.guardian.co.uk/world/2013/mar/27/greenland-halts-oil-drilling-licences (last accessed 4 April 2018).

407 Ibid. This issue related to the hunting and fishing activities of the Kalaallit, Inughuit and Tunumiit peoples.

408 Nunavut was formerly part of the Northwest Territories.

409 Government of Canada, Minister of Indian Affairs and Northern Development, '2012–2013 Call For Nominations – Arctic Islands Of Nunavut' (25 February 2013) at: http://www.aadnc-aandc.gc.ca/dam/dam-inter-hq-nog/staging/texte-text/rm_ri_ain_ain13_ain-nom2013_1360876151938_eng.pdf (last accessed 4 April 2018).

Devolution Agreement.[410] Regional governments will have a continuing interest in revenue from resources development, including royalties on oil and gas production. The development may also potentially increase the priority given to traditional hunting and fishing activities, and the priority given to the preservation of the environment.

Other Arctic regions have not significantly developed toward autonomy or independence, although this may develop in the future. The Russian government closed the Russian Association of Indigenous Peoples of the North (RAIPON) for a six-month period in 2012. RAIPON is Russia's permanent participant on the Arctic Council, representing its Arctic indigenous communities.[411] RAIPON received approval to renew its activities in 2013, following Russian Federal Ministry of Justice approval of amendments in the organisation's statutes.[412]

The significant issue for potential JDZs is how the interests and potential participation of indigenous groups should be addressed in the negotiation and implementation of JDZ agreements. This issue goes beyond revenue sharing and environmental concerns, to recognising the right for indigenous peoples to determine their future.

5.1.2 Developing Responses to Svalbard

There may be significant changes relating to the continental shelf resources of the Svalbard Islands. As discussed, Norway made a partial submission to the CLCS including the Western Nansen Basin region north of Svalbard.[413] The CLCS recommendation in 2009 was stated to be 'without prejudice to matters relating to delimitation between States, or application of other parts of the Convention or any other treaties.'[414] States may develop their responses to

410 Northwest Territories Land and Resources Devolution Agreement (25 June 2013) at: https://www.aadnc-aandc.gc.ca/eng/1390503182734/1390503256117 (last accessed 3 April 2018); and 'Canada's NW Territories to take control of its land, oil, gas' *Reuters Canada* (11 March 2013).

411 RAIPON had made a joint submission to the United Nations Human Rights Council in 2012; see 'NGO Submission to the Human Rights Council Universal Periodic Review Mechanism,' UPR 16th Session, April / May 2013, 9 October 2012, Submitted on behalf of the Russian Association of Indigenous Peoples of the North, the International Work Group for Indigenous Affairs, and the Institute for Ecology and Action Anthropology.

412 Atle Staalesen, 'Hard-fought new life for RAIPON', *Barents Observer* (15 March 2013) at: http://barentsobserver.com/en/society/2013/03/hard-fought-new-life-raipon-15-03 (last accessed 4 April 2018).

413 Commission on the Limits of the Continental Shelf (n. 236).

414 The CLCS recommendation therefore did not make any direct finding in relation to the Svalbard Treaty; however the 'without prejudice' recommendation was a recognition of

the issue of Svalbard resources in the next few years. Denmark, Iceland, Russia and Spain reacted to the Norwegian submission to the CLCS.[415] These responses did not dispute Norway's right to establish a continental shelf beyond 200 nautical miles around Svalbard, but they did not agree that Norway had an exclusive right to resources within that area.[416] This issue may potentially be referred to the ICJ or an arbitration tribunal. The potential outcome may be that a multilateral resource regime should apply, on the basis that the grant of sovereignty over Svalbard to Norway was conditional on sharing all the related resources.

5.1.3 Arctic Ocean Sanctuary

A significant development in 2013 was the proposal by Finland of a network of conservation areas in the Arctic region, including the seas surrounding the North Pole.[417] Neil Hamilton described the current circumstances of environmental protection in the Arctic Ocean region as 'the lowest level of protection of any ocean, in the most vulnerable place on Earth.'[418] The Finland strategy was followed by the European Union Resolution adopted in 2014, which included the establishment of a High Seas sanctuary about the North Pole.[419] The potential result, in the longer term, may be a ban on oil and gas development in the Arctic Ocean owing to increased environmental awareness. The growing concern in relation to environmental issues by NGOs, for example, was highlighted by the Greenpeace protest at the Prirazlomnoye offshore oil field in the Pechora Sea in 2013.[420] The prospect of an Arctic Ocean sanctuary

---

the related dispute: Summary of the Recommendations of the Commission on the Limits of the Continental Shelf In Regard To the Submission Made By Norway in Respect of Areas in the Arctic Ocean, the Barents Sea and the Norwegian Sea On 27 November 2006, 2, at: http://www.un.org/Depts/los/clcs_new/submissions_files/nor06/nor_rec_summ .pdf (last accessed 4 April 2018).

415 Torbjørn Pedersen and Tore Henriksen, 'Svalbard's Maritime Zones: The End of Legal Uncertainty?' (2009) 24 *International Journal of Marine and Coastal Law* 141, at p. 155.

416 Ibid., at p. 156. Pedersen and Henrikson note that there may be an issue of determining a maritime boundary between Svalbard and Norway, as the Svalbard Treaty would not apply to the Norwegian continental shelf and OCS.

417 Finland Government, *Finland's Strategy for the Arctic Region 2013* (Prime Minister's Office Publications, Helsinki: 2013).

418 Neil TM Hamilton, 'Go Finland! First Arctic nation to call for a global sanctuary around the North Pole', Greenpeace (4 September 2013) at: http://www.greenpeace.org/international/en/news/Blogs/makingwaves/go-finland-first-arctic-nation-to-call-for-a-/blog/46483/ (last accessed 4 April 2018).

419 European Parliament Resolution on the EU Strategy for the Arctic of 12 March 2014 (2013/2595) clause 38.

420 'Russians Fire Shots amid Greenpeace Arctic Protest' (n. 273).

may appear to be distant at present, given current development of offshore oil and gas by states including the United States and Russia;[421] however, in the longer term it remains a potentially game-changing event.

5.1.4 Arctic Council Development

David VanderZwaag has analysed proposals for a binding Arctic regime,[422] which included a framework treaty formalising the existing Arctic Council arrangements,[423] a regional seas agreement with annexes or protocols,[424] and a multilateral agreement dedicated to protecting the Arctic environment.[425] A regional management approach based on the Arctic Council faces challenges. Clive Schofield, Tavis Potts and Ian Townsend-Gault have commented that '... states with minimal territorial geopolitical interests but seeking opportunities in emerging economic sectors will continue to press for influence and action at the Arctic table.'[426] This interest of other states illustrates a potential challenge to a regional management approach, including the issue of whether to recognise any rights to resources for such states.

The Arctic Council has adopted a proactive approach towards the development of an effective governance regime. This trend has been accompanied by the establishment of a more effective administration following the establishment of the Standing Arctic Council Secretariat in Tromsø in 2013.[427] This very significant development was described by Byers as '... arguably transforming the Arctic Council from an inter-governmental forum into an international organisation.'[428] A recent analysis of the Arctic Council was made by Dodds

421 For a summary of current Arctic oil and gas developments see generally: Ernst & Young (n. 10).

422 Ibid., at p. 283.

423 Timo Koivurova, 'Alternatives for an Arctic Treaty – Evaluation and a new proposal' (2008) 17 *Review of European Community and International Environmental Law* 14.

424 Hans H Hertell, 'Arctic Melt: The Tipping Point for an Arctic Treaty' (2009) 21 *Georgetown International Environmental Law Review* 565.

425 Bonnie A. Malloy, 'On Thin Ice: How a Binding Treaty Regime Can Save the Arctic' (2010) 16 *Hastings West-Northwest Journal of Environmental Law & Policy* 471.

426 Clive H Schofield, Tavis Potts and Ian Townsend-Gault, 'Boundaries, Biodiversity, Resources, and Increasing Maritime Activities: Emerging Oceans Governance Challenges for Canada in the Arctic Ocean' (2009–2010) 34 *Vermont Law Review* 35.

427 Arctic Council, 'Arctic Council Secretariat in Tromsø opened by Arctic Ministers' (23 January 2013) at: https://www.arctic-council.org/index.php/en/our-work2/8-news-and-events/146-arctic-council-secretariat-in-tromso-opened-by-arctic-ministers (last accessed 4 April 2018).

428 Byers (n. 148) at p. 9.

in 2013,[429] including reference to the statement from the Ilulissat Declaration which highlighted the unique position of the five coastal states by virtue of their sovereignty in large areas of the Arctic Ocean.[430] Dodds summarised a dominant characteristic of the Arctic Council as 'openness to the future.'[431]

It is also arguable that the entry of significant observer states, as at March 2017 comprising France, Germany, the Netherlands, Poland, Spain, United Kingdom, China, Italy, Japan, Korea, Singapore and India, may potentially contribute to the emergence of the Arctic Council as effective for future Arctic governance.

The Arctic Council is developing significantly with the introduction of binding regimes, commencing with the Agreement on Cooperation on Aeronautical and Maritime Search and Rescue in the Arctic in 2011.[432] The Arctic Council will also develop with the implementation of the Arctic Marine Oil Pollution, Preparedness and Response (MOPPR) as the second binding Arctic Council regime,[433] and the Arctic Offshore Oil and Gas Guidelines.[434]

The principal potential change in the Arctic Ocean region would be a more comprehensive approach to oil and gas development, with new standards including rig platform and subsea equipment design and construction, rig platform and subsea equipment staff levels and training, and oil pollution emergency response, on a similar basis to the comprehensive regime adopted by the European Union.[435]

---

429 Klaus J Dodds, 'Anticipating the Arctic and the Arctic Council: pre-emption, precaution and preparedness' (2013) 49(2) *Polar Record* 193, at p. 194.

430 The statement was part of the Ilulissat Declaration as follows: "The Arctic Ocean stands at the threshold of significant changes. Climate change and the melting of ice have a potential impact on vulnerable ecosystems, the livelihoods of local inhabitants and indigenous communities, and the potential exploitation of natural resources. By virtue of their sovereignty, sovereign rights and jurisdiction in large areas of the Arctic Ocean the five coastal states are in a unique position to address these possibilities and challenges."

431 Dodds (n. 460) at p. 194.

432 2011 Agreement on Cooperation on Aeronautical and Maritime Search and Rescue (SAR) in the Arctic, at: http://www.treaty-accord.gc.ca/text-texte.aspx?id=105240 (last accessed 4 April 2018).

433 2013 Agreement on Cooperation on Marine Oil Pollution, Preparedness and Response in the Arctic, at: http://www.arctic-council.org/index.php/en/document-archive/category/425-main-documents-from-kiruna-ministerial-meeting (last accessed 4 April 2018).

434 Arctic Council, 'Arctic Offshore Oil and Gas Guidelines' (n.d.) at: https://oaarchive.arctic-council.org/handle/11374/62 (last accessed 4 April 2018).

435 European Union, *Directive 2013/30/EU of the European Parliament and of the Council of 12 June 2013 on safety of offshore oil and gas operations and amending Directive 2004/35/EC*, OJ L 178/66. The European Union measures include, for example, the design of rigs, missing from IMO regulations such as MARPOL, and a comprehensive liability regime, missing from UNCLOS: European Commission, 'Proposal for a Regulation Of The

5.2 *Arctic Ocean Environment*

Climate change in the form of global warming is potentially the greatest game changer in the Arctic Ocean region. In the longer time frame of 20 or 30 years, for example, the potential effect of global warming may be that there is little, or no, Arctic sea ice. Such a development would reduce the present difficulty of oil and gas development; however, this would also mean that risks of oil pollution increase as the level of oil and gas development increases. Current research also provides strong evidence for a current trend of significantly reducing Arctic Ocean ice. Research using the European Space Agency's *CryoSat-2* satellite, for example, has demonstrated a significant decline in Arctic Ocean ice extent. The research indicates that the summer minimum in Arctic sea ice is one-fifth of the level in 1980.[436] Global temperatures currently appear to be increasing as a result of carbon dioxide and other greenhouse gas emissions, and the consequential trapping of the sun's energy in the earth's atmosphere.[437]

Environmental concerns have also been highlighted by the *Deepwater Horizon* oil spill in the Gulf of Mexico off the United States.[438] The flow of crude oil into the ocean was estimated at up to 60,000 barrels per day as at

European Parliament and of the Council on safety of offshore oil and gas prospection, exploration and production activities' COM(2011) 688, at: https://euoag.jrc.ec.europa.eu/files/attachments/osd_final_eu_directive_2013_30_eu1.pdf (last accessed 4 April 2018), and European Commission, 'Commissioner Oettinger welcomes political agreement on offshore legislation', IP/13/149 (Press Release, 21 February 2013) at: http://europa.eu/rapid/press-release_IP-13-149_en.htm (last accessed 4 April 2018).

436 Seymour W Laxon, Katharine A Giles, Andy L Ridout et al, 'CryoSat-2 estimates of Arctic sea ice thickness and volume' (2013) 40 *Geophysical Research Letters* 732.

437 The primary reference for the current status of climate change is the Intergovernmental Panel on Climate Change ('IPCC'), which was established in 1988 by the United Nations Environment Programme ('UNEP') and the World Meteorological Organization (WMO) to provide the world with a clear scientific view on the current state of climate change and its potential environmental and socio-economic consequences. Significant reports issued by the IPCC include 'Climate Change 2007: Synthesis Report – An Assessment of the Intergovernmental Panel on Climate Change' (2008) Intergovernmental Panel on Climate Change, at: https://www.ipcc.ch/pdf/assessment-report/ar4/syr/ar4_syr_full_report.pdf (last accessed 4 April 2018), and Intergovernmental Panel on Climate Change, 'Working Group I Contribution to the IPCC Fifth Assessment Report, Climate Change 2013: The Physical Science Basis' (n. 8).

438 The oil spill commenced on April 20, 2010 following a methane gas explosion and resulting fire on the Deepwater Horizon semi-submersible mobile offshore drilling unit. The accident resulted in loss of life of 11 oil workers on the rig and an uncontrolled release of crude oil at a depth of 5,000 feet from the ocean surface. The accident occurred 41 miles from the coast in the United States EEZ adjoining the state of Louisiana in the Gulf of Mexico.

18 June 2010.[439] The limited effectiveness of the response to the oil spill provides strong support for the prevention of certain oil and gas activities at the current state of technological development. The oil spill may have been a contributing factor to the decision by Shell to suspend oil and gas development in the Beaufort and Chukchi Seas in 2013, until safety measures are improved.[440] Several incidents have also highlighted the importance of the prevention and control of pollution. In particular, oil spills may not disperse in Arctic waters for a very long period, and environmental damage can therefore be potentially very high.[441] There is a related issue concerning the actual effectiveness of environmental provisions.[442]

The principal issue of supervision relates to the enforcement of a regional prevention and response code. The Arctic Council in 2013 concluded the MOPPR. The JDZ should refer to compliance with Arctic Council environmental protection measures, such as those contained in the MOPPR, as a binding condition of JDZ approval and continued operations.[443] JDZ agreements in the Arctic Ocean region should incorporate effective measures for responses to oil spills, for example by incorporating the MOPPR measures in Arctic Ocean JDZs. One measure that should be included in JDZ Agreements is the requirement for oil company standby emergency resources, and effective pooling of these resources with other oil companies in the JDZ, and other oil companies in nearby oil and gas fields. Compliance by oil companies should also be subject to environmental audit, such as analysis by environment services groups of large accounting firms, to ensure that measures undertaken by oil companies and contractors continue to meet agreed contract standards.[444] The

439 Flow Rate Technical Group (FRTG), 'Press Briefing by National Incident Commander June 18, 2010', Deepwater Horizon Incident Joint Information Centre, Press Release (18 June 2010).

440 'Shell suspends Arctic drilling for 2013', *BBC* (27 February 2013) at: http://www.bbc.co.uk/news/business-21609892 (last accessed 1 April 2018). One potential outcome of an effective prevention, response and liability regime may be to influence oil and gas companies to focus on less environmentally risky projects in Arctic regions, such as a focus on gas development, compared to oil development, until such time as environmental protection measures are fully effective.

441 World Wildlife Fund (WWF) International Arctic Programme, *Oil Spill Response Challenges in Arctic Waters* (2007) 7.

442 Tina Hunter, 'The Montara oil spill and the marine oil spill contingency plan: Disaster response or just a disaster?' (2010) 24(2) *Australian and New Zealand Maritime Law Journal* 46.

443 Arctic MOPPR (n. 89).

444 Claude Duval, Honoré Le Leuch, André Pertuzio et al, *International Petroleum Exploration and Exploitation Agreements: Legal, Economic and Policy Aspects* (Barrows Company Incorporated, New York: 2009) 398.

choice of petroleum law in a JDZ agreement is also significant to provide an effective regulatory regime. One approach to provide for clear application of state environmental laws may be the use of each state's petroleum regime for bilateral JDZs in the Arctic region on their respective side of the median line of the JDZ.

The BIICL Model refers to environmental standards; however, there may be new standards introduced after the effective date of the JDZ agreement. An ambulatory interpretation approach should be used, which would provide for incorporation of future environmental standards as they are developed. The VCLT may potentially apply to the interpretation of a JDZ agreement as discussed; however, it does not provide for either static or ambulatory methods of interpretation. A JDZ agreement should therefore adopt an ambulatory approach to require the application of environmental standards at the date of the JDZ and future environmental standards.

There should be strict liability of oil companies and all contractors for the full amount of environmental clean-up costs, on a similar basis to Greenland oil and gas contracts.[445] The liability should apply to pollution from oil installations, and also from ships such as oil tankers. The required financial resources of oil company consortiums to meet the potential costs under the guarantees for environmental liability should therefore be set at a significant level. For example, BP has reported total costs of USD 61.6 billion with respect to the *Deepwater Horizon* offshore oil spill.[446] An alternative method is a fund which provides for the costs of remediating oil spills. The Arctic Council has not introduced such a measure as at April 2018, and it appears likely to be difficult to establish a fund at the necessary levels. The environmental provisions of a JDZ may include environment or pollution guarantees, which may be given by the oil company, its parent company and third-party financial institutions to guarantee to pay costs in the event of a major environmental incident. Specific insurance cover against events such as oil spills may also be a condition of the development agreement.[447]

445 This is based on the terms of Licence No 09/98 for Exploration for and Exploitation of Hydrocarbons for an Offshore Area West of Sisimiut in West Greenland, Mineral Resources Administration for Greenland (29 June 1998) at: http://www.geus.dk/ghexis/pdf/sislic.pdf (last accessed 4 April 2018).

446 Ed Crooks, 'BP draws line under Gulf spill costs', *Financial Times* (15 July 2016) at: https://www.ft.com/content/ff2d8bcc-49e9-11e6-8d68-72e9211e86ab (last accessed 4 April 2018).

447 Duval, Le Leuch, Pertuzio et al (n. 475) at p. 160.

5.3 *Oil and Gas Development and Energy Alternatives*

The introduction of JDZs can be prompted by oil and gas discoveries in disputed regions. The Thailand/Cambodia overlapping claim region is an example of significant oil discoveries in the disputed region leading to the adoption of the Thailand/Cambodia MOU. The likelihood of oil and gas may also lead to a full boundary agreement. The 2010 Barents Sea Treaty[448] was made in a region likely to have significant oil and gas resources. Oil and gas discoveries may lead to interest in a JDZ where the countries concerned are unwilling to give up coastal state sovereign rights over the ocean region, but have sufficiently good political relations to consider a JDZ as an interim solution to a maritime boundary dispute.

Improved pollution-control technology may also promote JDZs. There are likely to be improvements in pollution control arising from lessons learned from the *Deepwater Horizon* oil spill. The Shell Arctic drilling programme in 2012 included, for example, a containment dome directed at controlling a *Deepwater Horizon*-type oil spill.[449] There has also been comment that the dispersal chemicals used in the oil spill provided the appearance of cleaned coastline while actually causing the oil to sink below the surface.[450] Future research may indicate a preference for oil collection by methods such as 'skimming,' based on devices attached to ships to remove oil or oil/water mixtures. Other technological developments may include improvements in oil-spill detection, involving improvements in satellite, vessel, and aircraft-mounted oil-pollution detection radar.[451]

The further development of other sources of energy may, however, potentially reduce the pressure for development of offshore oil and gas from the Arctic Ocean region. This may include the further development of alternative

---

448 Treaty Between the Kingdom of Norway and the Russian Federation Concerning Maritime Delimitation and Cooperation in the Barents Sea and the Arctic Ocean, 2791 *UNTS* I-49095.

449 United States Department of the Interior, 'Review of Shell's 2012 Alaska Offshore Oil and Gas Exploration Program" (8 March 2013) 17, at: http://www.doi.gov/news/pressreleases/department-of-the-interior-releases-assessment-of-shells-2012-arctic-operations.cfm (last accessed 4 April 2018).

450 There are also concerns that the 'Corexit 9500' dispersant used by BP was potentially a toxic chemical; see Parliament of the United Kingdom, 'UK Deepwater Drilling – Implications of the Gulf of Mexico Oil Spill – Energy and Climate Change' (n.d.) at: http://www.publications.parliament.uk/pa/cm201011/cmselect/cmenergy/450/45012.htm (last accessed 4 April 2018).

451 'Detecting oil spills, Trouble beneath the ice', *The Economist* (1 December 2012) at: http://www.economist.com/news/technology-quarterly/21567196-energy-technology-oil-exploration-moves-arctic-new-methods-are-being (last accessed 4 April 2018).

sources of energy such as wind, solar, and wave power. These sources of energy may significantly decline in cost, and may potentially replace oil and gas in the longer term. These developments also relate to other sources of oil and gas. The primary current development is the use of hydraulic fracturing technology, or 'fracking'. This process generally uses water to increase fractures in rocks such as shale, allowing the recovery of oil and gas trapped in pores within the rocks.[452] Oil and gas prices also affect the potential for JDZs. There has been a substantial reduction in oil prices owing, in part, to the state of the world economy, and in part to the discovery of new sources of oil and gas, such as fracking and shale oil. A continued low oil price may delay or cancel oil exploration in regions such as the Arctic Ocean, which would have substantially higher production costs than other sources of oil.[453]

The greatest potential change may result from the introduction of more extensive measures to reduce carbon emissions to reduce the process of global warming. The process of reducing carbon emissions is principally based on the United Nations Framework Convention on Climate Change (UNFCCC),[454] the related 1997 Kyoto Protocol,[455] and the 2015 Paris Agreement.[456] The international measures to address global warming are essentially based on member state commitments to binding targets to reduce greenhouse gas emissions.[457] It has also been argued that there should be no further hydrocarbon exploitation in the Arctic if increases in global warming are to be kept within 2°C.[458] These measures may promote the reduced use of oil and gas as energy sources, and their replacement with alternative energy sources with lower greenhouse gas emissions.[459]

---

452 United States production of gas from shale rock was reported to have reduced gas prices from USD 13 per million British thermal units (BTU) in 2008, to USD 1–2 per million BTU in 2012; see 'Deep sigh of relief – The shale gas and oil bonanza is transforming America's energy outlook and boosting its economy', *The Economist* (16 March 2013); and International Energy Agency, *World Energy Outlook – Executive Summary* (2012) 7.

453 'Sheiks v Shale', *The Economist* (6 December 2014) 13.

454 United Nations Framework Convention on Climate Change, 1771 *UNTS* 107 (UNFCCC).

455 1998 Kyoto Protocol to the United Nations Framework Convention on Climate Change, 2303 *UNTS* 148 (*Kyoto Protocol*).

456 2015 Paris Agreement, C.N.63.2016.Treaties-XXVII.7.d (12 December 2015) at: https://treaties.un.org/doc/Publication/CN/2016/CN.63.2016-Eng.pdf (last accessed 4 April 2018).

457 Shaw (n. 393) at p. 880.

458 C McGlade and P Etkins, 'The Geographical Distribution of Fossil Fuels unused when limiting Global Warming to 2° C' (2015) 517 *Nature* 187.

459 JDZs may still be required to peacefully resolve competition for other resources. One example may be rare-earth elements (REE), particularly in a longer time frame such as 50 or 100 years. 'In a hole? Demand for some rare-earth elements could rapidly outstrip supply' (n. 6). There may also be competition over other resources in the Arctic Ocean region.

6 Conclusions

The use of JDZs based on their potential to resolve resource conflicts is supported by state practice in adopting JDZs. In the Arctic Ocean and surrounding region, this includes the examples of the Svalbard Treaty as early as 1920,[460] and the Iceland/Norway Agreement in the Jan Mayen Island area in 1981.[461] JDZs have, however, been unsuccessful in the absence of continued political support by one of the respective states. The principal examples are the 1995 United Kingdom/Argentina Joint Declaration relating to the South West Atlantic, and more recently the stalling in development of the 2008 Japan/China JDZ, owing to the dispute over the Senkaku Islands (Diaoyu Islands).

JDZs continue to be relevant as potential solutions because UNCLOS does not resolve all potential disputes over maritime boundaries, including the circumstances where maritime boundary disputes have arisen, such as claims based on the extension of the continental shelf rather than equidistance, the interpretation of rights granted under historic treaties, the effect to be given to islands, and the sovereignty over land masses or islands. A significant strength of UNCLOS dispute-resolution provisions is that the ICJ, ITLOS and arbitration panels can make a determination on such issues. The reputation of the ICJ and arbitral panels is such as to expect a determination to achieve an equitable result. These determinations may, however, result in an 'all or nothing' outcome for the respective state parties.

JDZs may allow joint development of oil and gas resources in several Arctic Ocean regions. JDZs may therefore provide solutions allowing joint development for:

- The United States/Canada maritime boundary in the Beaufort Sea and Arctic Ocean as a bilateral JDZ;
- The United States/Russia maritime boundary in the Bering and Chukchi Seas and the Arctic Ocean as a bilateral JDZ;
- Norway's Svalbard Islands-related continental shelf and OCS in the Greenland and Norwegian Seas and the Arctic Ocean as a form of multilateral JDZ; and
- The potential overlap in the central Arctic Ocean between the United States, Canada, Denmark and Russia, where equidistance lines from the respective coasts extend beyond the North Pole.

A form of multilateral development will also apply in the Central Arctic and Norwegian Sea, with the three likely zones under the multilateral regime of

460 Svalbard Treaty (n. 212).

461 Norway/Iceland Agreement (n. 318).

the Area under UNCLOS Part XI comprising the Central Bering Sea Doughnut Hole, the Barents Sea Loophole, and the Norwegian Sea Banana Hole.

The future adoption of JDZs in the Arctic Ocean region is subject to potential game-changing events. These events may include the full independence of Greenland, increased autonomy in regions including Canada's Northwest Territories and Nunavut, political developments relating to the Svalbard Islands, the potential for a future Arctic Ocean Sanctuary, the potential effects of climate change, future serious oil spills in polar or other regions, and the potential for substantially improved pollution control measures. The significance of JDZs, however, is their use, in a substantial number of cases, to resolve competing claims to maritime regions and related resources, and on this basis JDZs can provide solutions to maritime boundary disputes in the Arctic Ocean region.

Bibliography

Abrahamson, John, *Tolley's International Taxation of Upstream Oil and Gas* 2nd Edition (LexisNexis, London: 2017).

Allain, Monique Andree, 'Canada's Claim To The Arctic: A Study In Overlapping Claims To The Outer Continental Shelf' (2011) 42 *Journal of Maritime Law and Commerce* 1.

Amos, Howard, 'Arctic Treaty with Norway Opens Fields', *Moscow Times* (7 July 2011) at: http://old.themoscowtimes.com/business/article/arctic-treaty-with-norway-opens-fields/440178.html (last accessed on 3 April 2018).

Anderson, DH, 'Denmark (Greenland) – Iceland', Report Number 9–22', in Jonathan I Charney and Robert W Smith (eds), *International Maritime Boundaries* Vol 4 (Martinus Nijhoff, Dordrecht/London: 2002) 2941.

Anderson, DH, 'Iceland-Norway (Jan Mayen), Report Number 9–4', in Jonathan I Charney and Lewis M Alexander (eds), *International Maritime Boundaries* Vol 2 (Martinus Nijhoff, Dordrecht/Boston: 1993) 1755.

Anderson, DH, 'Denmark (Greenland) – Norway (Jan Mayen), Report Number 9–19', in Jonathan I Charney and Lewis M Alexander (eds), *International Maritime Boundaries* Vol 3 (Martinus Nijhoff, Dordrecht/Boston: 1998) 2507.

Anderson, DH, 'The Status under International Law of the Maritime Areas around Svalbard' (2009) 40(4) *Ocean Development and International Law* 373.

Arctic Council, 'Arctic Council Secretariat in Tromsø opened by Arctic Ministers' (23 January 2013) at: https://www.arctic-council.org/index.php/en/our-work2/8-news-and-events/146-arctic-council-secretariat-in-tromso-opened-by-arctic-ministers (last accessed on 4 April 2018).

Arctic Council, 'RAIPON's Activities Suspended', Indigenous Peoples Secretariat (17 November 2012) at: http://www.arcticpeoples.org (last accessed on 4 April 2018).

Arctic Council, 'Senior Arctic Officials (SAO) Report to Ministers', Nuuk, Greenland, (May 2011).

Arctic Council, 'The Arctic Ocean Review Project, Phase II Report 2011–2013', Protection of the Arctic Marine Environment Working Group, at: http://www.arctic-council.org/index.php/en/oceans/arctic-ocean-review/396-phase-ii-of-the-arctic-ocean-review-project (last accessed on 4 April 2018).

ArcticEcon, 'Iceland's New Era of Offshore Exploration' (14 January 2013) at: https://arcticecon.wordpress.com/category/iceland/ (last accessed on 3 April 2018).

Armstrong, Patrick, and Vivian Forbes, 'The Falkland Islands and their Adjacent Maritime Area' (1995) 2(3) *IBRU Maritime Briefing* 27.

Baker, James S., and Michael Byers, 'Crossed Lines: The Curious Case of the Beaufort Sea Maritime Boundary Dispute' (2012) 43(1) *Ocean Development and International Law* 70.

Bastida, Ana E, Adaeze Ifesi-Okoye, Salim Mahmud et al, 'Cross-border unitization and joint development agreements: an international law perspective' (2006–2007) 29 *Houston Journal of International Law* 355.

Benitah, Marc, 'Russia's Claim in the Arctic and the Vexing Issue of Ridges in UNCLOS' (2007) *American Society of International Law ASIL Insight* 11, at: http://www.asil.org/insights/2007/11/insights071108.html (last accessed on 1 March 2018).

Bird, Kenneth J et al, 'Circum-Arctic Resource Appraisal: Estimates of Undiscovered Oil and Gas North of the Arctic Circle', *U.S. Geological Survey Fact Sheet* 2008–3049, at: http://pubs.usgs.gov/fs/2008/3049/ (last accessed on 1 March 2018).

Blinn, Keith W et al, *International Petroleum Exploration and Exploitation Agreements* (The Barrows Company Inc, New York: 1986).

Boczek, Boleslaw A, *International Law: A Dictionary* (Scarecrow Press, Lanham: 2005).

Boswell, Randy, 'Ocean Survey Looks Promising for Arctic Sovereignty Effort' *National Post* (16 May 2008).

British Broadcasting Corporation, 'Argentina Ends Falklands Oil Deal', *BBC News* (28 March 2007) at: http://news.bbc.co.uk/2/hi/americas/6501693.stm (last accessed on 4 April 2018).

British Broadcasting Corporation, 'Shell suspends Arctic drilling for 2013', BBC (27 February 2013) at: http://www.bbc.co.uk/news/business-21609892 (last accessed on 4 April 2018).

Brown, ED, *Sea-Bed Energy and Minerals: The International Legal Regime*; Vol 1 The Continental Shelf (Martinus Nijhoff Publishers, Dordrecht: 1992).

Browne, Marjorie Ann, 'The Law of the Sea Convention and U.S. Policy', *CRS Issue Brief for Congress* (10 February 2005) at: http://www.fas.org/sgp/crs/row/IB95010.pdf (last accessed on 1 March 2018).

Byers, Michael, *International Law and the Arctic* (Cambridge University Press, Cambridge: 2013).

Caracciolo, Ida, 'Unresolved controversy: the legal situation of the Svalbard Islands maritime areas; an interpretation of the Paris Treaty in light of UNCLOS 1982' (paper presented at International Boundary Research Unit Conference, The State of Sovereignty, Durham, 2009) at: http://www.dur.ac.uk/resources/ibru/conferences/sos/ida_caracciolo_paper.pdf (last accessed on 1 March 2018).

Churchill, RR, and AV Lowe, *The Law of the Sea* 3rd ed (Manchester University Press, Manchester: 1999).

Churchill, Robin and Geir Ulfstein, *Marine Management in Disputed Area: The Case of the Barents Sea* (Routledge, London: 1992).

Clapham, Andrew, *Brierly's Law of Nations, An Introduction to the Role of International Law in International Relations* 7th ed (Oxford University Press, Oxford: 2012).

Clinton, William Jefferson, 'Message from the President of the United States and Commentary Accompanying the United Nations Convention on the Law of the Sea and the Agreement Relating to the Implementation of Part XI Upon their Transmittal to the United States Senate for its Advice and Consent' (1994) *Georgetown International Environmental Law Review* 7.

Coates, Ken S, P Whitney Lackenbauer, William R Morrison et al, *Arctic Front – Defending Canada in the Far North* (Thomas Allen & Son, Toronto: 2008).

Crooks, Ed, 'BP draws line under Gulf spill costs', *Financial Times* (15 July 2016) at: https://www.ft.com/content/ff2d8bcc-49e9-11e6-8d68-72e9211e86ab (last accessed on 1 March 2018).

Davenport, Tara, 'Joint Development in Asia: Lessons for sustainable Peace in the South China Sea' (Paper presented at the 8th Asian Law Institute Conference, Kyushu, 26 and 27 May 2011) at http://cil.nus.edu.sg/wp/wp-content/uploads/2011/06/TaraDavenport-ASLI-Joint-Development-as-a-tool-for-peace-4-April-2011-v2.pdf (last accessed on 1 March 2018).

Deepwater Horizon Incident Joint Information Centre, 'Press Briefing by National Incident Commander June 18, 2010', Flow Rate Technical Group (FRTG), (Press Release, 18 June 2010).

Department of Foreign Affairs and Trade (Australia), 'Continental Shelf Submission of Australia, Executive Summary' AUS-DOC-ES (2004) at: http://www.un.org/Depts/los/clcs_new/submissions_files/aus04/Documents/aus_doc_es_web_delivery.pdf (last accessed on 3 April 2018).

Dodds, Klaus J, 'Anticipating the Arctic and the Arctic Council: pre-emption, precaution and preparedness' (2013) 49(2) *Polar Record* 193.

Duval, Claude, Honoré Le Leuch, André Pertuzio et al, *International Petroleum Exploration and Exploitation Agreements: Legal, Economic and Policy Aspects* (Barrows Company Incorporated, New York: 2009).

Ernst & Young, 'Arctic Oil and Gas (2013)' at: http://www.ey.com/Publication/vwLUAssets/Arctic_oil_and_gas/$FILE/Arctic_oil_and_gas.pdf (last accessed on 4 April 2018).

European Commission, 'Commissioner Oettinger welcomes political agreement on offshore legislation', IP/13/149 (Press Release, 21 February 2013), at: http://europa.eu/rapid/press-release_IP-13-149_en.htm (last accessed on 4 April 2018).

Falkland Islands Department of Mineral Resources, 'Exploration History' at: http://www.bgs.ac.uk/falklands-oil/exp_history.html (last accessed on 4 April 2018).

Falkland Oil and Gas Limited, 'Falkland Oil and Gas Limited, Investor Presentation', (November 2011) at: http://www.fogl.com/fogl/uploads/companypresentations/CorporatePresentationnonUSviewer.pdf (last accessed on 1 March 2018).

Finland Government, 'Finland's Strategy for the Arctic Region 2013' (Prime Minister's Office Publications, Helsinki: 2013).

Fox, Hazel et al, *Joint Development of Offshore Oil and Gas, A Model Agreement for States for Joint Development with Explanatory Commentary* (British Institute of International and Comparative Law, London: 1989).

Fox, Hazel et al, *Joint Development of Offshore Oil and Gas, A Model Agreement for States for Joint Development with Explanatory Commentary* Vol 2 (British Institute of International and Comparative Law, London: 1990).

Gazprom, 'Prirazlomnoye oil field', at: http://www.gazprom.com/about/production/projects/deposits/pnm/ (last accessed on 4 April 2018).

Górski, Tomasz, 'A Note on Submarine Ridges and Elevations with Special Reference to the Russian Federation and the Arctic Ridges' (2009) 40(1) *Ocean Development and International Law* 51.

Government of Argentina, 'The Question of the Malvinas Islands', Ministry of Foreign Affairs (2012) at: http://www.consuladoargentinoenmiami.org/userfiles/Folleto_CuestionMalvinas_INGLES.pdf (last accessed on 1 March 2018).

Government of Australia, 'Timor-Leste and Australia Joint Petroleum Development Area' (n.d.) at: https://industry.gov.au/resource/UpstreamPetroleum/Pages/Timor-LesteandAustraliaJointPetroleumDevelopmentArea.aspx (last accessed on 2 March 2018).

Government of Canada, 'Oil and Gas Dispositions' (n.d.) at: https://www.aadnc-aandc.gc.ca/dam/dam-inter-hq-nog/staging/texte-text/le_mp_bsmd_pg_1371579383933_eng.pdf (last accessed 3 April 2018).

Government of Canada, 'Partial Submission of Canada to the Commission on the Limits of the Continental Shelf regarding its continental shelf in the Atlantic Ocean, Executive Summary' (2013) 3 at: http://www.un.org/depts/los/clcs_new/submissions_files/can70_13/es_can_en.pdf (last accessed 3 April 2018).

Government of Canada, 'Preliminary Information concerning the outer limits of the continental shelf of Canada in the Arctic Ocean' (6 December 2013) at: http://www.un.org/depts/los/clcs_new/submissions_files/preliminary/can_pi_en.pdf (last accessed on 1 March 2018).

Government of Canada, 'Beaufort Sea' (n.d.) at: http://publications.gc.ca/Collection-R/LoPBdP/BP/bp322-e.htm (last accessed on 4 April 2018).

Government of Canada, Fisheries and Oceans Canada, 'Canada's Submission to the Commission on the Limits of the Continental Shelf Under the United Nations Convention on the Law of the Sea (The 'Continental Shelf Program')' (22 September 2009) at: http://www.dfo-mpo.gc.ca/ae-ve/evaluations/09–10/6b060-eng.htm (last accessed on 4 April 2018).

Government of Canada, Foreign Affairs and International Trade Canada, 'Canada and Kingdom of Denmark Reach Tentative Agreement on Lincoln Sea Boundary' Press Release (28 November 2012) at: https://www.canada.ca/en/news/archive/2012/11/canada-kingdom-denmark-reach-tentative-agreement-lincoln-sea-boundary.html (last accessed on 4 April 2018).

Government of Canada, Minister of Indian Affairs and Northern Development, '2012–2013 Call For Nominations – Arctic Islands Of Nunavut' (25 February 2013) at: http://www.aadnc-aandc.gc.ca/dam/dam-inter-hq-nog/staging/texte-text/rm_ri_ain_ain13_ainnom2013_1360876151938_eng.pdf (last accessed on 4 April 2018).

Government of Greenland, 'Licence No 09/98 for Exploration for and Exploitation of Hydrocarbons for an Offshore Area West of Sisimiut in West Greenland', Mineral Resources Administration for Greenland (29 June 1998) at: http://www.geus.dk/ghexis/pdf/sislic.pdf (last accessed on 4 April 2018).

Government of Russia, 'Statement Made by the Deputy Minister for Natural Resources of the Russian Federation During Presentation of the Submission Made by the Russian Federation to the Commission on 28 March 2002', Doc. CLCS/31 (5 April 2002).

Government of the United Kingdom, 'UK Deepwater Drilling – Implications of the Gulf of Mexico Oil Spill – Energy and Climate Change' (n.d.) at: http://www.publications.parliament.uk/pa/cm201011/cmselect/cmenergy/450/45012.htm (last accessed on 4 April 2018).

Government of the United States, 'Message From The President Of The United States Transmitting the Agreement Between The United States Of America And The Union of Soviet Socialist Republics on the Maritime Boundary, with Annex, Signed at Washington, June 1, 1990,' United States Department of State (26 September 1990) at: http://www.state.gov/documents/organization/125431.pdf (last accessed on 4 April 2018).

Government of the United States, 'Review of Shell's 2012 Alaska Offshore Oil and Gas Exploration Program", United States Department of the Interior (8 March 2013) at: http://www.doi.gov/news/pressreleases/department-of-the-interior-releases-assessment-of-shells-2012-arctic-operations.cfm (last accessed on 4 April 2018).

Governor of Svalbard, 'Historical background', The Governor of Svalbard (n.d.) at: http://www.sysselmannen.no/en/Toppmeny/About-Svalbard/Historical-background/ (last accessed on 4 April 2018).

Gray, David, 'Canada's Unresolved Maritime Boundaries' (1997) *IBRU Boundary and Security Bulletin* 61.

Green, Arthur R, and Anatoly A Kaplan, 'The Geological Framework and Hydrocarbon Potential of Sedimentary Basins of the Arctic' in *Proceedings of the Twelfth World Petroleum Congress* Vol 2 (1987) 79.

Hamilton, Neil TM, 'Go Finland! First Arctic nation to call for a global sanctuary around the North Pole', Greenpeace (4 September 2013) at: http://www.greenpeace.org/international/en/news/Blogs/makingwaves/go-finland-first-arctic-nation-to-call-for-a-/blog/46483/ (last accessed on 1 March 2018).

Hartmann, Jacques, 'Canada and Denmark reach agreement on the Lincoln Sea Boundary', *EJIL: Talk!* (Blog of the *European Journal of International Law*) (10 January 2013) at: http://www.ejiltalk.org/canada-and-denmark-reach-agreement-on-the-lincoln-sea-boundary/ (last accessed on 4 April 2018).

Headland, RK, 'Ships (icebreakers) which have reached the North Pole', Scott Polar Research Institute, University of Cambridge (17 August 2017) at: http://www.spri.cam.ac.uk/resources/infosheets/14.html (last accessed on 1 March 2018).

Henriksen, Tore, and Geir Ulfstein, 'Maritime Delimitation in the Arctic: The Barents Sea Treaty' (2011) 42 *Ocean Development and International Law* 1.

Hertell, Hans H, 'Arctic Melt: The Tipping Point for an Arctic Treaty' (2009) 21 *Georgetown International Environmental Law Review* 565.

Hunter, Tina, 'The Montara oil spill and the marine oil spill contingency plan: Disaster response or just a disaster?' (2010) 24(2) *Australian and New Zealand Maritime Law Journal* 46.

Intergovernmental Panel on Climate Change, 'Climate Change 2007: Synthesis Report – An Assessment of the Intergovernmental Panel on Climate Change' (2008) at: http://www.ipcc.ch/publications_and_data/publications_and_data_reports.htm#1 (last accessed on 4 April 2018).

Intergovernmental Panel on Climate Change, 'Working Group I Contribution to the IPCC Fifth Assessment Report, Climate Change 2013: The Physical Science Basis', at: http://www.ipcc.ch (last accessed on 4 April 2018).

International Boundaries Research Unit (Durham University), 'Argentina and UK claims to maritime jurisdiction in the South Atlantic and Southern Oceans' (n.d.) at: https://www.dur.ac.uk/ibru/resources/south_atlantic/ (last accessed on 4 April 2018).

International Boundaries Research Unit (Durham University), 'Details Emerge of the 2009 Brunei-Malaysia Maritime Agreement' (2010) International Boundaries Research Unit, at http://www.dur.ac.uk/ibru/news/boundary_news/?itemno=10047&rehref=%2Fibru%2Fnews%2F&resubj=Boundary+news%20Headlines (last accessed on 4 April 2018).

International Boundaries Research Unit (Durham University), 'Maritime jurisdiction and boundaries in the Arctic Region' (n.d.) at: http://www.dur.ac.uk/resources/ibru/arctic (last accessed on 4 April 2018).

International Boundaries Research Unit (Durham University), 'Russia submits new Arctic Ocean claim' (4 November 2014) at: https://www.dur.ac.uk/ibru/news/boundary_news (last accessed on 2 March 2018).

International Energy Agency, 'World Energy Outlook – Executive Summary' (2012) at: https://www.iea.org/weo/ (last accessed on 4 April 2018).

International Law Association, 'Outer Continental Shelf Committee of the International Law Association (ILA) Berlin Conference 2004', at: http://www.ila-hq.org/en/committees/index.cfm/cid/33 (last accessed on 4 April 2018).

International Seabed Authority, 'Decision of the Assembly relating to the regulations on prospecting and exploration for poly-metallic nodules in the Area' (13 July 2000) UN Doc. ISBA/6/A/18.

International Seabed Authority, 'Deep Seabed Minerals Contractors' (n.d.) at: https://www.isa.org.jm/deep-seabed-minerals-contractors (last accessed on 4 April 2018).

Koivurova, Timo, 'Alternatives for an Arctic Treaty – Evaluation and a new proposal' (2008) 17 *Review of European Community and International Environmental Law* 14.

Lagoni, Rainer, 'Oil and Gas Deposits across National Frontiers' (1979) 73(2) *American Journal of International Law* 215.

Laxon, Seymour W, Katharine A Giles, Andy L Ridout et al, 'CryoSat-2 estimates of Arctic sea ice thickness and volume' (2013) 40 *Geophysical Research Letters* 732.

Lodge, Michael, 'The International Seabed Authority and Deep Seabed Mining' (May 2017) LIV, No 1 and 2 *UN Chronicle* at: https://unchronicle.un.org/article/international-seabed-authority-and-deep-seabed-mining (last accessed on 10 April 2018).

Macnab, Ron, Paul Neto and Rob van de Poll, 'Cooperative Preparations for Determining the Outer Limit of the Juridical Continental Shelf in the Arctic Ocean' (2001) *Boundary and Security Bulletin* 86.

Macnab, Ron, 'Submarine Elevations and Ridges: Wild Cards in the Poker Game of UNCLOS Article 76' (2008) 39(2) *Ocean Development and International Law* 223.

Malaysia Thailand Joint Authority, 'Chronicle' (n.d.) at: https://www.mtja.org/chronicle.php (last accessed on 4 April 2018).

Malloy, Bonnie A, 'On Thin Ice: How a Binding Treaty Regime Can Save the Arctic' (2010) 16 *Hastings West-Northwest Journal of Environmental Law & Policy* 471.

Manicom, James, 'China's Claims to an Extended Continental Shelf in the East China Sea: Meaning and Implications' (2009) 9(14) *China Brief* 9.

Manicom, James, 'Disputed Claims in the East China Sea', interview by Chris Acheson, The National Bureau of Asian Research, Seattle (25 July 2011) at: http://www.nbr.org/research/activity.aspx?id=159 (last accessed on 1 March 2018).

Marcussen, Christian et al, 'Exploring for extended continental shelf claims off Greenland and the Faroe Islands – geological perspectives' (2004) 4 *Geological Survey of Denmark and Greenland Bulletin* 61.

McDorman, Ted L, *Salt Water Neighbors – International Ocean Relations between the United States and Canada* (Oxford University Press, New York/Oxford: 2009).

McGlade, C, and P Etkins, 'The Geographical Distribution of Fossil Fuels unused when limiting Global Warming to 2° C' (2015) 517 *Nature* 187.

Meese, SA, 'The Legal Regime Governing Polymetallic Sulfide Deposits' (1986) 17 *Ocean Development and International Law* 131.

Miles, E, *Global Ocean Politics* (Martinus Nijhoff, The Hague: 1998).

Miyoshi, Masahiro, and Clive H Schofield (eds), 'The Joint Development of Offshore Oil and Gas in relation to Maritime Boundary Delimitation' (1999) 2(5) *IBRU Maritime Briefing* 3.

Miyoshi, Masahiro, 'Seabed Petroleum in the East China Sea: Law of the Sea Issues and the Prospects for Joint Development' (n.d.) at: http://www.wilsoncenter.org/sites/default/files/Miyoshi_Masahiro.pdf (last accessed on 1 March 2018).

Molenaar, EJ, 'Fisheries Regulation in the Maritime Zones of Svalbard' (2012) 27 *International Journal of Marine and Coastal Law* 3.

National Oceanic and Atmospheric Administration (United States of America), 'Federal and State Offshore Oil & Gas Leases, Beaufort & Chukchi Seas' (n.d.) at: www.nmfs.noaa.gov/pr/pdfs/permits/openwater/map.pdf (last accessed on 4 April 2018).

National Oceanography Centre, 'Continental Shelf Beyond 200 Miles' (n.d.) at: http://www.unclosuk.org/submissions-currently-united-nations (last accessed 4 April 2018).

Nelson, L Dolliver M, 'Reflections on the 1982 Convention on the Law of the Sea' in David Freestone, Richard Barnes and David Ong, *The Law of the Sea: Progress and Prospects* (Oxford University Press, Oxford: 2006) 35.

Nguyen, Lan-Anh T, 'Joint Development between Malaysia and Vietnam' (n.d.) at: https://cil.nus.edu.sg/wp-content/uploads/2011/06/Session-5-Lan-Anh-Joint-development-between-Malaysia-Vietnam-pdf.pdf (last accessed on 1 March 2018).

Ong, David M, '1979 and 1990 Malaysia Thailand Joint Development Agreements: A Model for International Legal Cooperation in Common Offshore Petroleum Deposits?' (1999) 14(2) *International Journal of Marine and Coastal Law* 213.

Onorato, William T, 'Apportionment of an International Common Petroleum Deposit' (1977) 26(2) *International and Comparative Law Quarterly* 324.

Oude Elferink, Alex G, and Donald R Rothwell (eds), *The Law of the Sea and Polar Maritime Delimitation and Jurisdiction* (Martinus Nijhoff, The Hague: 2005).

Oude Elferink, Alex G, and Donald R Rothwell, 'Challenges for Polar Maritime Delimitation and Jurisdiction: The Current Regime and Its Prospects' in Alex G Oude

Elferink and Donald R Rothwell (eds), *The Law of the Sea and Polar Maritime Delimitation and Jurisdiction* (Martinus Nijhoff, The Hague: 2001) 337.

Oude Elferink, Alex G, 'Arctic Maritime Delimitations: The Preponderance of Similarities with Other Regions' in Alex G Oude Elferink and Donald R Rothwell (eds), *The Law of the Sea and Polar Maritime Delimitation and Jurisdiction* (Martinus Nijhoff, The Hague: 2001) 179.

Oude Elferink, Alex G, 'Current Legal Developments, Denmark/Iceland/Norway' (1998) 13(4) *International Journal of Marine and Coastal Law* 607.

Oude Elferink, Alex G, 'Submissions of Coastal States to the CLCS in Cases of Unresolved Land or Maritime Disputes' in Myron H Nordquist, John N Moore and Tomas H Heidar (eds), *Legal and Scientific Aspects of Continental Shelf Limits* (Martinus Nijhoff, Leiden/Boston: 2004) 263.

Oude Elferink, Alex G, *The law of maritime boundary delimitation: a case study of the Russian Federation* (Martinus Nijhoff, Dordrecht/Boston: 1994).

Oxman, Bernard H, 'The 1994 Agreement and the Convention' (1994) 88(4) *American Journal of International Law* 687.

Park, Chris and Michael Allaby, *A Dictionary of Environment and Conservation* 3rd ed (Oxford University Press, Oxford: 2017).

Pedersen, Torbjørn, and Tore Henriksen, 'Svalbard's Maritime Zones: The End of Legal Uncertainty?' (2009) 24 *International Journal of Marine and Coastal Law* 141.

Pedersen, Torbjørn, 'Denmark's Policies toward the Svalbard Area' (2009) 40(4) *Ocean Development and International Law* 319.

Pedersen, Torbjørn, 'The Svalbard Continental Shelf Controversy: Legal Disputes and Political Rivalries' (2006) 37(3) *Ocean Development and International Law* 339.

Pharand, Donat, 'Canada's Arctic Jurisdiction in International Law' (1982–1983) 7 *Dalhousie Law Journal* 315.

Pratt, Martin, 'Maritime Jurisdiction and Boundaries in the Arctic Region', International Boundaries Research Unit (n.d.) at: http://www.dur.ac.uk/ibru/resources/arctic/ (last accessed on 1 March 2018).

Reuters Canada, 'Canada's NW Territories to take control of its land, oil, gas' (11 March 2013).

Revenue Watch Institute, 'Timor Sea Designated Authority First Tranche Petroleum and Profit Oil' (2009) at: http://www.revenuewatch.org/training/resource_center/timor-sea-designated-authority-first-tranche-petroleum-and-profit-oil (last accessed on 4 April 2018).

Rigzone, 'Russians Fire Shots amid Greenpeace Arctic Protest' (18 September 2013) at: http://www.rigzone.com/news/oil_gas/a/129108/Russians_Fire_Shots_amid_Greenpeace_Arctic_Protest (last accessed on 4 April 2018).

Rothwell, Donald R, and Tim Stephens, *The International Law of the Sea* 2nd ed (Bloomsbury, Oxford: 2016).

Rothwell, Donald R, 'Building on the Strengths and Assessing the Challenges: The Role of Law of the Sea Institutions' (2004) 35 *Ocean Development and International Law* 131.

Rothwell, Donald R, 'Issues and Strategies for Outer Continental Shelf Claims' (2008) 23 (2008) *International Journal of Marine and Coastal Law* 185.

Rothwell, Donald R, *The Polar Regions and the Development of International Law* (Cambridge University Press, Cambridge: 1996).

Royal Dutch Shell, 'Shell Updates on Alaska Exploration', Shell Global (28 September 2015) at: https://www.shell.com/media/news-and-media-releases/2015/shell-updates-on-alaska-exploration.html (last accessed on 4 April 2018).

Russian Association of Indigenous Peoples of the North, 'NGO Submission to the Human Rights Council Universal Periodic Review Mechanism,' UPR 16th Session, April / May 2013, 9 October 2012, Submitted on behalf of the Russian Association of Indigenous Peoples of the North, the International Work Group for Indigenous Affairs, and the Institute for Ecology and Action Anthropology, at http://www.raipon.info/en/component/content/article/8-news/91-ngo-submission-to-the-human-rights-council-universal-periodic-review-mechanism.html (last accessed on 4 April 2018).

Scandinavian Oil and Gas Magazine, 'Transocean's Deepwater Horizon drills world's deepest O&G well' (3 September 2009) at: http://www.scandoil.com/moxie-bm2/news/transoceans-deepwater-horizon-drills-worlds-deepes.shtml (last accessed on 4 April 2018).

Schofield, Clive H, and Ian Townsend-Gault, 'Choppy Waters Ahead in 'a sea of peace cooperation and friendship'? – Maritime Joint Development in the East China Sea' (Paper presented at the International Boundary Research Unit Conference, Durham, 2 April 2009) at: http://www.dur.ac.uk/ibru/conferences/sos/programme/2_april/track2_session4/#schofield (last accessed on 1 March 2018).

Schofield, Clive H, 'Minding the Gap: The Australia-East Timor Treaty on Certain Maritime Arrangements in the Timor Sea (CMATS)' (2007) 22(2) *International Journal of Marine and Coastal Law* 201.

Schofield, Clive H, Tavis Potts and Ian Townsend-Gault, 'Boundaries, Biodiversity, Resources, and Increasing Maritime Activities: Emerging Oceans Governance Challenges for Canada in the Arctic Ocean' (2009–2010) 34 *Vermont Law Review* 35.

Scovazzi, Tullio, 'The Baseline of the Territorial Sea: The Practice of Arctic States' in AG Oude Elferink and DR Rothwell (eds), *The Law of the Sea and Polar Maritime Delimitation and Jurisdiction* (Martinus Nijhoff, The Hague: 2001) 69.

Shaw, Malcolm N, *International Law* 6th ed (Cambridge University Press, Cambridge: 2008).

Staalesen, Atle, 'Hard-fought new life for RAIPON', *Barents Observer* (15 March 2013) at: http://barentsobserver.com/en/society/2013/03/hard-fought-new-life-raipon-15-03 (last accessed on 4 April 2018).

Symmons, Clive, 'The Irish Partial Submission to the Commission on the Limits of the Continental Shelf in 2005: A Precedent for Future Such Submissions in the Light of the "Disputed Areas" Procedures of the Commission?' (2006) 37 *Ocean Development and International Law* 3.

The Economist, 'Deep sigh of relief – The shale gas and oil bonanza is transforming America's energy outlook and boosting its economy', *The Economist* (16 March 2013).

The Economist, 'Detecting oil spills, Trouble beneath the ice', *The Economist* (1 December 2012) at: http://www.economist.com/news/technology-quarterly/21567196-energy-technology-oil-exploration-moves-arctic-new-methods-are-being (last accessed on 4 April 2018).

The Economist, 'In a hole? Demand for some rare-earth elements could rapidly outstrip supply', *The Economist* (17 March 2012) at: http://www.economist.com/node/21550243 (last accessed on 4 April 2018).

The Economist, 'Sheiks v Shale', *The Economist* (6 December 2014) 13.

The Economist, 'The Arctic – Gold Rush under the Ice', *The Economist* (3 August 2007).

The Guardian, 'Greenland halts new oil drilling licences', *The Guardian* (27 March 2013) at: http://www.guardian.co.uk/world/2013/mar/27/greenland-halts-oil-drilling-licences (last accessed on 4 April 2018).

The Japan Times, 'East China Sea Gas Fields', *The Japan Times* (19 June 2008) at: http://www.japantimes.co.jp/text/nn20080619a1.html (last accessed on 4 April 2018).

Total S.A., 'Yamal LNG, A Gas Project Like No Other' (n.d.) at: https://www.total.com/en/media/video/yamal-lng-gas-project-no-other (last accessed on 2 March 2018).

Townsend-Gault, Ian, 'Joint Development of Offshore Mineral Resources – Progress and Prospects for the Future' (1988) 12(3) *Natural Resources Forum* 275.

Townsend-Gault, Ian, 'The Impact of a Joint development Zone on Previously Granted Interests', in Hazel Fox (ed), *Joint Development of Offshore Oil and Gas, A Model Agreement for States for Joint Development with Explanatory Commentary* Vol 2 (British Institute of International and Comparative Law, London: 1990) 106.

Treves, T, 'La Nona Sessione della Conferenza sul Diritto del Mare' (1980) 63 *Rivista di Diritto Internazionale* 432.

Triggs, Gillian, and Dean Bialek, 'The New Timor Sea Treaty and Interim Arrangements for Joint Development of Petroleum resources of the Timor Gap' (2002) 3 *Melbourne Journal of International Law* 322.

Turner, John, 'Accession to the 1982 Law of the Sea Convention and Ratification of the 1994 Agreement Amending Part XI of the Law of the Sea Convention,' Testimony before the Senate Environment and Public Works Committee, 23 March 2004, Senate Treaty Document 103–39; Senate Executive Report 108–10.

Ulfstein, Geir, *The Svalbard Treaty: From* Terra Nullius *to Norwegian Sovereignty* (Scandinavian University Press, Oslo: 1995).

United Nations Division for Ocean Affairs and the Law of the Sea, 'Chronological Lists of Ratifications of, Accessions and Successions to the Convention and Related

Agreements' (3 April 2018) at: http://www.un.org/Depts/los/reference_files/chronological_lists_of_ratifications.htm (last accessed on 4 April 2018).

United Nations Division for Ocean Affairs and the Law of the Sea, 'Preliminary information indicative of the outer limits of the continental shelf beyond 200 nautical miles' (8 December 2017) at: http://www.un.org/Depts/los/clcs_new/commission_preliminary.htm (last accessed on 4 April 2018).

United Nations, 'Settlement of Disputes Mechanism' United Nations Division for Ocean Affairs and the Law of the Sea, at http://www.un.org/Depts/los/settlement_of_disputes/choice_procedure.htm (last accessed on 4 April 2018).

United Nations, 'Settlement of Disputes Mechanism' United Nations Division for Ocean Affairs and the Law of the Sea, at http://www.un.org/Depts/los/settlement_of_disputes/choice_procedure.htm (last accessed on 4 April 2018).

United Nations, 'Statement by the Chairman of the Commission on the Limits of the Continental Shelf on the progress of work in the Commission' United Nations Commission on the Limits of the Continental Shelf (24–28 June 2002) UN Doc. CLCS/34, 33.

United States Department of State, 'Status of Wrangel and Other Arctic Islands', Fact Sheet, Bureau of European and Eurasian Affairs, Washington (20 May 2003) at: https://2001–2009.state.gov/p/eur/rls/fs/20922.htm (last accessed on 4 April 2018).

United States Department of State, 'Bering Sea' (n.d.) at: http://www.state.gov/p/eur/rls/fs/128740.htm (last accessed on 4 April 2018).

United States Government, 'Law of the Sea Convention Letters of Transmittal and Submittal and Commentary', United States Department of State, Dispatch Volume 6, Supplement Number 1, February 1995, at http://dosfan.lib.uic.edu/ERC/briefing/dispatch/1995/html/Dispatchv6Sup1.html (last accessed on 4 April 2018).

University of Aberdeen, 'Capturing the Energy', University of Aberdeen – Politics Economics and Society (n.d.) at: http://www.capturing-the-energy.org.uk/frigg/ (last accessed on 2 March 2018).

Valencia, Mark and Masahiro Miyoshi, 'Southeast Asian Seas: Joint Development of Hydrocarbons in overlapping Claim Areas' (1996) 16 *Ocean Development and International Law* 211.

Verville, Elizabeth G, 'United States – Soviet Union', Report Number 1–6, in Jonathan I Charney and Lewis M Alexander (eds), *International Maritime Boundaries* Vol 1 (Martinus Nijhoff, Dordrecht/Boston: 1993) 447.

Walde, TW, and Andrew McHardy, 'Introductory Note, Argentina – United Kingdom: Joint Declaration on Cooperation over Offshore Activities in the South West Atlantic' (1996) 35 *International Legal Materials* 301.

Weber, Mel, 'Defining the Outer Limits of the Continental Shelf across the Arctic Basin: The Russian Submission, States' Rights, Boundary Delimitation and Arctic Regional Cooperation' (2009) 24 *International Journal of Marine and Coastal Law* 653.

World Wildlife Fund, 'Oil Spill Response Challenges in Arctic Waters' World Wildlife Fund International Arctic Programme (2007).

Yee, Sienho, 'Conciliation and the 1982 UN Convention on the Law of the Sea' (2013) 44(4) *Ocean Development and International Law* 321.

Yoshida, Reiji and Shinichi Terada, 'Japan, China strike deal on gas fields' *The Japan Times* (19 June 2008) at: https://www.japantimes.co.jp/news/2008/06/19/national/japan-china-strike-deal-on-gas-fields/ (last accessed on 3 April 2018).

Yu, Jiang (Chinese Foreign Ministry), 'China, Japan reach principled consensus on East China Sea issue' Press Release (18 June 2009) at: http://www.china-embassy.org/eng/fyrth/t466632.htm (last accessed on 1 March 2018).

www.ingramcontent.com/pod-product-compliance
Lightning Source LLC
Chambersburg PA
CBHW071353230926
51846CB00002B/536
9789004380097